INSIGHT POCKET GUIDE

SRI Lanka

APA PUBLICATIONS L
Part of the Langenscheidt Publishing Group

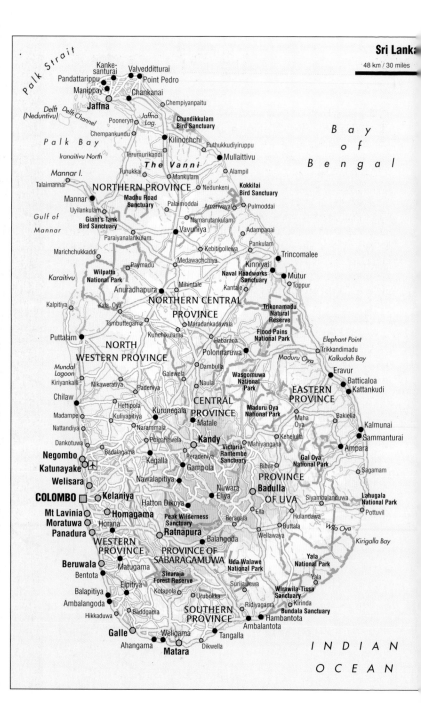

Sri Lanka

48 km / 30 miles

introduction

Welcome

This guidebook combines the interests and enthusiasms of two of the world's best-known information providers: Insight Guides, who have set the standard for visual travel guides since 1970, and Discovery Channel, the world's premier source of non-fiction television programming. Its aim is to help visitors get the most out of Sri Lanka during a short stay with the help of a series of carefully crafted itineraries devised by Insight's correspondent in Sri Lanka, Vijitha Yapa. Intent on revealing the rich variety of the country's landscapes and attractions, he explores many of the lesser known corners of the island as well as the more traditional tourist hot-spots. British-born author and travel writer, Royston Ellis, a resident of Sri Lanka for 20 years, has also contributed his knowledge and experience of the country. The sights of teeming Colombo, the palm-fringed beaches of the south, the hill resorts of Nuwara Eliya and Kandy, the wildlife sanctuary of Yala and the great monuments of Sri Lanka's ancient kingdoms are all covered in the pages of this reader-friendly guide.

Supporting the itineraries are sections on the history and culture of Sri Lanka and options for shopping, eating out and nightlife, as well as a detailed practical information section which includes a list of recommended hotels.

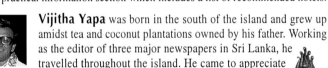

Vijitha Yapa was born in the south of the island and grew up amidst tea and coconut plantations owned by his father. Working as the editor of three major newspapers in Sri Lanka, he travelled throughout the island. He came to appreciate first-hand the country's raw beauty, and also witnessed the tragic civil strife and conflict that has torn the island apart over the past few years. Although Yapa has taken the routes described in this book many times over, he continues to be amazed by the diversity of Sri Lanka. He hopes that your journey will be just as memorable.

contents

EXCURSIONS

These trips are ideal for those who wish to see Sri Lanka's natural beauty. The selection covers diverse options that take you from beach to hill country.

LEISURE ACTIVITIES

CALENDAR OF EVENTS

PRACTICAL INFORMATION

MAPS

INDEX AND CREDITS

Pages 2/3: tea plantation
Pages 8/9: Kataragama Festival

History *& Culture*

The romantics summed up the shape and substance of Sri Lanka best when they called it 'The Teardrop of India'. For if the face of the great Indian subcontinent had ever shed a tear of joy, one which froze in mid-air as it fell from her cheek, that teardrop would undoubtedly have become the island of Sri Lanka. To Sri Lankans, this is the original Garden of Eden.

They proudly point to places named after Adam to prove their case. The 2,224-metre (7,297-ft) Adam's Peak is claimed by all four major religions of Sri Lanka as a holy mountain, and is much better known than Pidurutalagala which, at 2,524m (8,281 ft), is the highest mountain on the island. On a trek to the summit of Adam's Peak you will find a motley assortment of Buddhist, Hindu, Christian and Muslim pilgrims. The narrow stretch of rocks and islands between Sri Lanka and India – seen in recent NASA photos as the remains of a bridge – is believed to be part of Adam's Bridge. God is said to have broken it into pieces after banishing Adam from the Garden of Eden so that he could never return.

Whatever the veracity of that story, the earliest reference to the island is found in the great Hindu epic the *Ramayana*. Rawana, the 10-headed king of Lanka, seeking to avenge an insult to his sister, travelled to India in a winged carrier called the Dandumonara and abducted Sita, wife of Rama. The enraged Rama enlisted the help of the monkey god, Hanuman, defeated Rawana and reclaimed Sita. Rawana Ella (Rawana Falls) and Sita Eliya (Sita's Light) in the hill country are associated with that 5,000-year-old story and today still attract large numbers of visitors.

Jewels and Spices

To Asians, the island has always been known as Lanka. But not so to the Arabs or Westerners who braved high seas to visit this faraway land of jewels and spices. Taprobane, Zeilan, Serendib and Ceylon are only a few examples of the island's plethora of former names.

Sri Lanka has made fascinating contributions to the richness of the English language. The word 'serendipity' – the faculty of making unexpected discoveries by accident – was coined

Left: a Buddhist procession
Right: a stone guard in Polonnaruwa

by Horace Walpole in his fairy tale, *The Three Princes of Serendib*. And the word 'anaconda' (a native South American snake) comes from the Sinhala word, *henakanda*, used to describe a snake with a thick body. Strangely, no anacondas have ever been sighted on the island.

Early Origins

According to local legend, the Sinhala people are descended from a lion (*sinha*). The *Mahavamsa* (Great Chronicle), the history of the island written by Buddhist monks over a period of some centuries and tracing the course of events over the past 2,500 years, dates the beginning of Sri Lanka's history with the arrival of Prince Vijaya in 544BC. Vijaya, who would one day become Lanka's first king, landed in Lanka from India with some 700 followers on the day that Lord Buddha died in India.

Legend has it that his father, a minor king named Sinhabahu, had been sired by a lion. This is the most likely explanation for the symbol of the lion on the Sri Lankan flag. Vijaya grew up to be a rebellious young man. When he did not mend his youthful ways, despite repeated warnings, his father decided to banish him. Vijaya set sail and docked on a stretch of land in Lanka which he called Tambapanni, on account of its copper-coloured sand. The *Mahavamsa* recounts that Kuveni, an enchantress, attempted to bewitch him. Protected by a charmed thread, Vijaya managed to outwit her. He made Kuveni his queen, but after a few years he decided to banish her to the forest. Her children became the Veddhas (Aborigines living in Sri Lanka), whose descendants still hunt with bows and arrows.

Historical research confirms that the original Indo-Aryan settlers in Lanka were indeed from northern India. They mingled with the indigenous races, the *Yaksa* and the *Naga*, and introduced their Prakit language, which eventually evolved into Sinhalese.

Embracing Buddhism

During the 3rd century BC, the ruler of Sri Lanka, King Devanampiyatissa, embraced Buddhism following a meeting with Venerable Mahinda, the son of the Emperor of India, Ashoka. The island's capital, Anuradha-

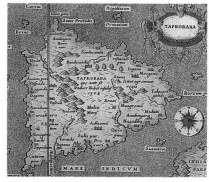

Above: the holy site of Adam's Peak
Right: a 1576 map of Sri Lanka

pura, founded in 437BC, soon underwent a remarkable transformation with Buddhist *dagobas*, incredibly elaborate feats of engineering that attract admirers even today, rising into the sky. Theravada Buddhism is still the primary influence in the lives of the Sinhalese, who form approximately 70 percent of the population.

In 205BC, however, the Tamil warrior Elara defeated the Sinhala king and was able to take complete control of Anuradhapura. It was not until 161BC that King Dutugemunu rallied the support of the people and defeated Elara. More than 2,000 years later, Dutugemunu is still the most important national hero among the Sinhalese community.

Invasions Galore

Constant invasions from south India eventually led to the abandonment of Anuradhapura. Over the following centuries, a succession of kings shifted their capitals to various cities. Perhaps the most significant was Polonnaruwa, close to the eastern coast, where the ruins, in a better state of preservation than those in Anuradhapura, tell an incredible story of a proud people. Parakramabahu the Great – who ruled the island from Polonnaruwa between 1153 and 1156 – built, among other things, the Parakramabahu Samudraya, which covers 2,400 ha (5,928 acres) and remains the largest and most spectacular of Sri Lanka's *wewa* or irrigation tanks. Parakramabahu declared that not one drop of water should pass into the Indian Ocean without it being of some service to humanity. During his short but important reign, Sri Lanka even began to export rice.

When the Portuguese reached Colombo in 1505, the king was only 13km (8 miles) away at the capital, Kotte, the site of the present parliament and the island's new capital. He was informed that some visitors in iron clothes (suits of armour), who ate stones (white bread), drank blood from bottles (wine) and had sticks that made noises like thunder (firearms), were asking to meet him.

The king ordered the foreigners to be brought to him, but instructed the guards to take them on a roundabout route so that they would think Kotte to be some distance from Colombo. The enthusiastic guides took several weeks to bring in the Portuguese, but the game was up when the commander, who was waiting in Colombo, fired cannons to signal his concern at their lengthy absence. The Portuguese realised they had been tricked. To this day, the phrase in Sinhala (the language of the Sinhalese) for 'taking someone for a ride' is 'like taking the Portuguese to Kotte'.

Divide and Rule

At first, the Portuguese were interested only in wresting what they could of the spice and cinnamon trade from Arab merchants and the Sinhalese rulers of Kotte. To this end they took full advantage of local rivalries. They

Above: the puppet king Dom Jão Dharmapala

installed Dom Jão Dharmapala as a puppet ruler, first in Kotte and then in Colombo. In 1617, as a result of a Portuguese treaty with the ruler of Kandy, the king's son, Rajasinghe II, formed his own alliance with the Dutch. The Portuguese turned from trade to military matters. They also introduced Roman Catholicism and today a number of Sri Lankans, even those not descended from the Portuguese, have Portuguese names. (Sri Lankans with Portuguese or Dutch ancestors are known as Burghers and have a reputation for being a charming, fun-loving people.)

The Dutch

The Dutch influence stemmed from their development of the spice trade in the East Indies; now, in return for getting rid of the Portuguese, they wanted a monopoly of the island's spice trade. The Dutch captured Galle from the Portuguese in 1641 and in 1656 took over the fort in Colombo. The Dutch, to the dismay of Kandy's king, stayed on the island, developing the infrastructure with canals and roads and making enormous profits from cinnamon. They built coastal villas, many of which can still be seen today, and inspired furniture makers to use elaborate designs. Their presence finally came to an end in 1796 when, as a result of events in Europe's Napoleonic wars, they were forced to cede their possessions in Ceylon to the British. In 1815, following a duplicitous deal with Kandy's prime minister, the British took control of Kandy and thus the whole of the island. Ceylon became part of the British empire.

The pace for development was set by the governor, Sir Edward Barnes, in the 1820s and 1830s. He initiated a massive road-building programme and opened up the island to British settlers. Cash crops were introduced, the economy was transformed and with it the lifestyle of the Ceylonese, as they had become known. Coffee replaced cinnamon as the main export and this was itself replaced by tea from 1867. That was the year the first field of tea was planted by Scotsman James Taylor near Kandy. It was also the year that

the first train steamed into Kandy, heralding the beginning of a rail network throughout the country. This development led tea to become a profitable export as it could be transported speedily to Colombo for shipment to England.

Universal Suffrage

Prosperity created a new local aristocracy and encouraged aspirations in colonists and native inhabitants alike. Constitutional reform was introduced, and in 1931, only two years after the British themselves achieved universal adult suffrage, full democracy was introduced in Ceylon. Following in India's footsteps, Ceylon gained independence, but without bloodshed, on 4 February 1948.

Britain bequeathed a legacy of a parliamentary system of democracy and D.S. Senanayake took his place as he first prime minister after independence. In July 1960 Sirimavo Bandaranaike, widow of the assassinated prime minister, S.W.R.D. Bandaranaike, became the world's first woman prime minister. In 1978, a presidential system with members of parliament being elected on a proportional formula was introduced, with J.R. Jayewardene of the United National Party becoming executive president. Mrs Bandaranaike's daughter Chandrika Kumaratunga, of the People's Alliance, was elected president in 1994.

In 1983, simmering discontent by disaffected Tamils, banded together as the Liberation Tigers of Tamil Elam (LTTE), boiled over into an attack on government security personnel in Jaffna that killed 13 people. Two decades of fighting followed and at least 64,000 lives were lost. The disputed Jaffna peninsula was ruined and Colombo was hit by suicide attacks. In 2001, rebels launched an assault on the international airport. A year later a ceasefire was signed and appeared to be holding, if not exactly moving towards a long-term deal, when another disaster struck.

The Boxing Day tsunami of 2004, killed more than 30,000 Sri Lankans and displaced 100,000 more. As rebuilding began and millions of dollars worth of aid arrived, there was some hope of a new dawn in community relations. In August 2005, though, came a reminder of the bad old days, when Lakshman Kadirgamar, the foreign minister, was assasinated.

Left: Dutch invasion. **Above:** early Sinhalese
Right: former premier D.S. Senanayake

The Island's Geography

Sri Lanka has a land area of 65,610 sq km (25,332 sq miles), making it about the same size as Ireland. It is 445km (277 miles) long and 225km (140 miles) across at its widest point. The population is 20 million, with two-thirds of the people occupying about one-third of the land.

There are wide variations in climate – the higher you go, the cooler it gets. Nuwara Eliya, for example, enjoys permanent springtime with an average temperature of 16°C (61°F). Meanwhile, in Kandy 518 metres (1,700ft) above sea level, a Mediterranean summer reigns throughout the year. In Colombo the humidity can make it seem considerably hotter than the city's average temperature of 27°C (80°F). As a result of its proximity to the equator, Sri Lanka doesn't enjoy many seasonal changes other than those brought by the monsoons. Every year it is hit by two monsoons, coming from different directions at different times. Colombo and the southwest receive a drenching from April to October; while the east coast's wet season runs from November to January. Although there isn't really any twilight at this latitude, the sunsets are truly magnificent.

Much forestry was burned by the British, who wanted to plant coffee and later tea. But there are still substantial tracts of scrub jungle, rainforests and high-altitude cloud forests. The longest river, the Mahaweli, snakes its way from the central hills to Trincomalee in the east, where it empties into the Indian Ocean. Successive governments have ambitiously tried to tame the Mahaweli River, thereby perpetuating the resolve of King Parakramabahu not to waste one drop of water. In the 1980s, over US$2 billion was spent on building giant dams to tap the Mahaweli for hydroelectric and irrigation projects, and to divert the waters to arid areas.

The west and south coasts are low and fringed with coconut trees. As tourists discovered these stunning beaches, hotels of all shapes and sizes cropped up. Many were flattened by the tsunami of 2004, but the pace of reconstruction, in the commercial sector at least, has been rapid.

Above: a beach on the west coast

HISTORY HIGHLIGHTS

48BC Prince Vijaya arrives in Sri Lanka with 700 followers and becomes the island's first king. The dynasty lasts until 1815, with a total of 185 rulers.

380BC The island's first capital is established at Anuradhapura.

248BC King Devanampiyatissa converts to the Buddhist faith.

260BC Sangamitta, daughter of India's Emperor Ashoka, brings a cutting from the bo (*Ficus religiosa*) tree under which the Buddha gained enlightenment.

205BC The Indian warrior Elara captures Anuradhapura and rules for 44 years.

161BC Elara is defeated by King Dutugemunu, the greatest national hero of the majority Sinhala community.

AD993 The Cholas of south India capture Anuradhapura, and the capital is moved to Polonnaruwa.

1070 King Vijayabahu succeeds in driving out the Cholas.

1505 The Portuguese arrive and extract concessions from the King of Kotte.

1656 The Dutch oust the Portuguese and introduce Dutch law.

1796 The Dutch surrender their possessions on the island to the British.

1815 The last native king is captured at Kandy after the British conspire with his prime minister, ending 24 centuries of monarchy. For the first time, the whole island falls under foreign rule and becomes part of the British empire.

1832 A revised form of government under Sir Edward Barnes opens up the island to British settlers.

1867 Tea is grown commercially. Railways reach the hill country plantations.

1915 Riots on the centenary of the fall of Kandy are put down by the British, leading to radical protest movements.

1931 Universal franchise is granted.

1948 Ceylon granted independence. D.S. Senanayake becomes the first PM.

1956 The ruling United National Party is defeated at the polls and S.W.R.D. Bandaranaike becomes prime minister.

1959 Bandaranaike is assassinated.

1960 His widow, Sirimavo Bandaranaike, becomes world's first woman PM.

1965 Mrs Bandaranaike's government is defeated and Dudley Senananyake becomes prime minister.

1966 *Poya* (full moon) days are declared public holidays.

1970 Mrs Bandaranaike returns to power.

1972 The name 'Ceylon' is officially changed to Sri Lanka and a republican constitution is adopted.

1978 A new constitution introduces the office of executive president and brings in proportional representation. J.R. Jayewardene becomes the first president.

1983 The LTTE attack on the army sparks ethnic clashes and the intensification of separatist guerrilla activity.

1987 Indian peace-keeping troops arrive, but end up fighting Tamil separatists.

1989 Ranasinghe Premadasa is elected president.

1990 Indian troops leave Sri Lanka at President Premadasa's request.

1993 Premadasa is assassinated.

1994 Chandrika Bandaranaike Kumaratunga is elected president while her mother, Sirima Bandaranaike, becomes prime minister.

1995 Peace talks with LTTE representatives collapse.

1996 Sri Lanka's fledgling cricket team wins the World Cup.

1997 The LTTE is declared a terrorist organisation in the USA.

1999 Chandrika Bandaranaike Kumaratunga is re-elected as president.

2004 South Asian tsunami kills more than 30,000 Sri Lankans

2005 Aid effort continues, but ethnic tensions remain and foreign minister Lakshman Kadirgamar is assasinated.

Colombo
500 m / 550 yds

Itinerary 1
Itinerary 2
Itinerary 3
Itinerary 4
Itinerary 5

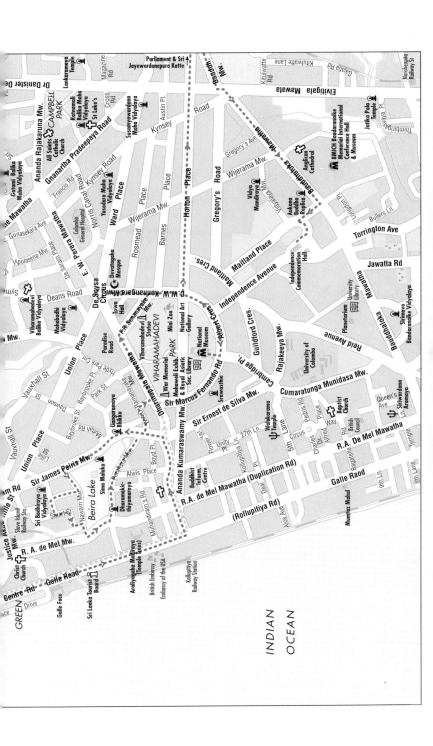

City Itineraries

As there is only one major airport on Sri Lanka, all visitors arrive via Bandaranaike International Airport, unless they're travelling by ship or yacht. The ferry between India and Sri Lanka has not been in operation since the early 1980s and the chances of it resuming are remote, until the railway link to Talaimannar Pier is restored in the island's north (it was destroyed by terrorist activity). The airport is located 32km (20 miles) from Colombo and the duration of your journey will depend on the time of day you are travelling. It usually takes an hour, but allow longer when travelling back towards the airport in case you are held up by queues of traffic at the airport security checkpoints. Other potential causes of delay all over Sri Lanka include narrow roads, crazy drivers and obstacles such as cows, dogs and unpredictable pedestrians. The majority of flights from the West arrive in the morning, while those from the East generally arrive and leave at night, when there is less traffic on the road.

The Road South

Facing the sea to the west, the port city of Colombo has expanded more northwards and southwards along the coast than eastwards inland. Its main artery is Galle Road, which stretches for a distance of 116km (72 miles) south to the port city of Galle. The city is divided into 15 numbered zones, though these are not necessarily geographically sequential. For instance, Colombo 5 and 6 are neighbours but 6 and 7 are 8km (5 miles) apart. The city's main commercial area is the Fort, which is dominated by the bustling harbour.

In theory all Colombo's streets have signposts in Sinhala, English and Tamil, but often it is more fruitful to search for the names of roads on shop signboards than on the streets. Some signs can be confusing as they retain old names of roads, leading cynics to say that Sri Lankans do not build new roads, they merely rename roads built by the British, with much longer titles. Thus, Parsons Road has been renamed Sir Chittampalam Gardiner Mawatha while Flower Road has become Sir Ernest de Silva Mawatha. The city's rickshaws have also adapted to changing times. Today they have a third wheel and the hard-pressed coolie has become a seated driver.

Left: a young vendor at Pettah market
Right: a typical cause of traffic jams

1. COLOMBO FORT *(see map, p18–19)*

A full-day walking tour of the city's major sights. Begin at the commercial hub called the Fort – though there is little evidence of any walls – where historical buildings abound.

Start in the Colombo Fort area, where three of the city's five-star hotels – the Intercontinental, the Hilton and the Galadari – are found. In front of Hotel Galadari on Lotus Road is the **Presidential Secretariat**, which used to house the parliament, until it moved, in 1982, to more spacious quarters in the island's new administrative capital, Sri Jayewardenepura Kotte. The Presidential Secretariat remains a high-security zone so, although there is no notice banning photography, be careful not to attract police attention.

A Historical Reminder

The **Fort**, the commercial area of Colombo, was defended in turn over the centuries by the Dutch, the Portuguese and the British. Some old cannons by the Presidential Secretariat still point out towards the sea – a reminder of the historical threat of invasion from the ocean. The security measures could lead you to think that there is still the possibility of attack from a foreign power. Due to the presence of a naval base, the Chaitya Road promenade alongside the Ceylon Continental Hotel is closed to

Above: the view south from the Fort
Left: the Lighthouse Clock Tower

city itineraries

motorists, but pedestrians can walk up to the lighthouse, which was once a very popular meeting place for lovers, and visit the Jayanthi Dagoba. This religious monument, built by the city's port workers in 1956 to commemorate the 2,500th year of Buddhism, can be seen from miles away if you come by sea: it stands 78 metres (256ft) high on a base of 156 steps. Inside, the dagoba features 12 bronze sculptures by the well-known Sri Lankan artist Ven Mapala-gama Vipulasura, 31 paintings of the Buddha's life and some interesting examples of verses from Sinhala literature.

The walk through the Fort starts at the roundabout opposite the Presidential Secretariat with a stroll towards the Clock Tower along Janadhipathi Mawatha. Hotel Ceylon Continental is to the left and on the right is the circular **Bank of Ceylon headquarters**. The latter building is thought to be tilting; some say it will one day become the country's answer to the Leaning Tower of Pisa. The bank has a convenient exchange counter for travellers' cheques and cash.

Just adjacent are the twin towers of the **World Trade Centre**, Colombo's tallest and most prestigious building, whose many offices include that of Sri Lankan Airlines. If you need to conduct some urgent business, the World Trade Centre rents out office space by the day. The deli market here is particularly popular in the evenings when people flock to enjoy the huge variety of food in what is a singular setting. In front of this, hidden by a cluster of trees, is a colonial building that once housed a Dutch hospital. Continue walking towards the Clock Tower. **Ceylinco Building** is on the right. Just inside its gate is a small memorial to the last Lankan king, Sri Wickrema Rajasinghe, who was imprisoned here by the British after being captured in Kandy in 1815.

Unique Lighthouse

The Lighthouse Clock Tower you have been using as a marker is on the spot where Janadhipathi Mawatha and Chatham Street meet. Probably the best-known landmark of the Fort, the tower, built in 1857, is the only lighthouse in the world that also tells the time in the middle of a busy street. Past the tower is the **President's House**, which is not accessible to the public for security reasons.

Janadhipathi Mawatha merges into Sir D.B. Jayatilleke Mawatha, where the **Premadasa & Co** gem shop sells an assortment of jewellery in beautiful designs. This, the banking district, is home to local and foreign banks, a number of airline offices and the country's six-storey Board of Investments building. The street is lined with formidable colonial buildings whose architecture is worth contemplating for a few minutes.

At the end of the street, near Seylan Bank, turn left to York Street, where you can change money without much hassle at the Bank of Ceylon's *bureau de change*. Nearby is the **Grand Oriental Hotel** (tel: 2448734), originally built in the mid-1850s as barracks for soldiers. Its 1991 refur-

Right: Presidential Secretariat

bishment retained its old charm. The Harbour Room is fun for dinner and to watch the passing ships, while the hotel's basement hosts a lively pub, the Tap Bar (from 11am), and the Blue Leopard nightclub.

About 23 metres (75ft) to the left of the Grand Oriental is the **Church of St Peter**, originally the reception and banquet hall of the Dutch governor's residence. First utilised as a church in 1804, its many plaques commemorate the colonial pioneers. Explain to the port security guards that you want to look at the church and, if you are lucky, the caretaker will show you around. Retrace your steps to the Grand Oriental and cross York Street to Leyden Bastion Road. Walk in the shade of the dilapidated colonial buildings opposite the port, turn right into the extension of Sir Baron Jayatilaka Mawatha and cross the road to the YMBA Building.

The Buddha's Serenity

Mind how you cross the street. Pedestrian crossings, described by some as merely yellow stripes which break the monotony of a black road, are seldom respected by motorists. Cynics say only a funeral procession will make Sri Lankans stop for pedestrians: the deceased might have died in a road accident. Inside the YMBA building, a serene statue of the Buddha beckons those seeking peace and tranquillity. As they leave flowers in front of the shrine, the devout often utter in Pali: 'Gaze upon these beautiful flowers, which in a few hours will wither away. Such is my own life.' Turn left at Bristol Street and walk to the new headquarters of the Commercial Bank. Nearly touching the walls of the bank is the **Delft Gateway**, built during the Dutch period of 1656–1796. The fort's ramparts were removed by the British in 1872 to accommodate an administrative building. There were two such gates at one time but no one seems to know what happened to the other.

Further down this road is the General Post Office and Philatelic Bureau, adjoining the YMCA.

Return to Jayatilaka Mawatha and cross York Street to **Cargills** and **Millers**, neighbouring department stores where the Colombo elite once shopped. Managed by a single conglomerate, the stores are a far cry from their former splendour. On the same road, the state-run **Laksala** is excellent for national souvenirs. A wide range of the island's handicrafts, such as giant carved masks and coconut-shell carvings, are displayed in Laksala's spacious surroundings. About 100 metres (330 ft) from Laksala, where York Street turns left, is the main entrance of the **Hilton Hotel**, where you might break for lunch at the Lotus Terrace. The daily buffet of Western, Chinese and Sri Lankan specialities is good value for money. After lunch, turn left outside the hotel and you will be at the busy junction of Lotus Road. If you turn left there you can reach the Ministry of Finance, the Presidential Secretariat and the seashore, with the Galadari Hotel on your left. Turn right and walk along Lotus Road to where it joins Olcott Mawatha.

Bargain At Any Price

On the right you will see a bazaar called the World Market, which is open throughout the day and early evening. Suit and dress materials are sold there, as well as an exciting array of goods, including leather bags, T-shirts and toys. Transactions should never be undertaken without bargaining, so don't pay the first price asked.

Nearby is the **Fort Railway Station**, the country's main rail terminal. Trains leave for all parts of the island, even the hill country of the interior. To visit the beach areas, book a seat on the *Ruhunu Kumari* train that departs at 4pm every day for Galle and Matara. Two trains a day with reserved and observation-car accommodation run to and from Kandy. The *Podi Menike* and *Udarata*

Menike trains to Badulla also have observation cars. Check times with the railway enquiry desk (tel: 2434215) or in *Travel Lanka* magazine, available free from the Sri Lanka Tourist Board information desk at 78 Stuart Place in Galle Road, opposite the Colombo Plaza Hotel. If you simply want to marvel at the activity in the station, buy a platform ticket for Rs4. The state-owned bus depot near the railway station serves most parts of the island. The buses of the private depot down the road reach their destinations faster because they race through traffic at breakneck speeds.

The little streets on the left lead into the heart of the **Pettah**, named after the Tamil word *pettai* ('old town') and corrupted by the British to Pettah. All roads lead to Main Street and each has a distinctive character. The first

Top Left: Colombo Fort railway station's impressive facade.
Left: Cargills department store. **Above:** facing the future

city itineraries

sells electrical goods and shoes, the second textiles and clothes, the third hardware, the fourth food items and the fifth wholesale goods and food. Take 1st Cross Street and turn right to Prince Street, which sells glass, mirrors and electrical items. The old post office in Prince Street is now the **Dutch Period Museum** (9am–5pm, closed Fri and public holidays; tel: 2448466; entrance fee), which exhibits a fine furniture collection.

If you are interested in buying music cassettes or CDs in Sinhala, Tamil or English, return to 1st Cross Street, turn right and then left on Keyzer Street (which specialises in household items) until you reach Malwatte Avenue (Front Street). Cassette prices are in the Rs120–180 range, depending on thelength and quality. Sinhala pop makes for easy listening, whereas Sri Lanka's indigenous *baila* music, though clearly influenced by Portuguese rhythms, has a distinctive style of its own.

Minarets Like Candy Bars

From here, continue on Malwatte Avenue till you reach the top of the road and turn right into Main Street by the Khan clock tower. Continue till you reach 2nd Cross Street and turn left to see the striking red-and-white **Pettah Mosque**. It is a pretty sight against the drab adjoining buildings, and the minarets look like candy bars. At the neighbouring 3rd Cross Street is the grey **Memm Harnafi Mosque**, which is architecturally more traditional.

Top: the harbour as seen by an 18th-century Dutch engraver
Above: Pettah Mosque

Return to Main Street, and continue till you reach **Kayman's Gate**. The word 'Kayman' comes from the Dutch *cayman* (crocodile) – there was a time when crocodiles gathered here to eat leftovers thrown out from the fort. The belfry to the right dates back to the Dutch period and could be the oldest Christian structure in Sri Lanka. The bell used to ring to indicate closing time for tipplers drinking at the local taverns.

At Kayman's Gate, turn right to Bodhiraja Mawatha (formerly Gas Works Street) to see the **Old Town Hall**. Originally built in 1873, it has been extensively restored and retains the high-roofed double portico which once gave access to horse-drawn carriages. It is still used as municipal offices. On the first floor you can see the meeting room where costumed mannequins recreate a 1906 meeting of town councillors. Adjoining the Old Town Hall is the **Colombo Municipal Council Museum**, where the exhibits include Sri Lanka's first printing machine (by Harrild & Sons of Fleet Works, London), drinking fountains and road rollers. Reflecting local history, the museum also contains the monument bequeathing the Galle Face promenade, built in 1856 by Governor Henry Ward, to the 'ladies and children of Colombo'.

Colourful Hindu Deities

Take a taxi or auto-rickshaw back to your hotel or, if you have the energy, continue the tour by returning to Kayman's Gate and going up **Sea Street**, the road where goldsmiths trade. These stores are popular with Sri Lankans and Indians, especially brides-to-be who come here to shop for gold jewellery. At the end of Sea Street you will see the beautiful ancient and new Hindu **Kathiresan temples**. There are more temples on Gintupitiya Street to the right. Hindu deities painted in various colours adorn the tall buildings. By the sea, just beyond the point where Sea Street joins St Anthony's Mawatha, the famous **Church of St Anthony** serves as a sanctuary, not only for Christians, but for anyone seeking solace. Every Tuesday, people of various faiths flock to the church to tap into the miraculous powers attributed to the saint. This sort of cross-worship happens a good deal in Sri Lanka. Among the devotees there will almost certainly be Hindus who worship down the road in Kotahena Street, where the **Muthumariamman Kovil** is dedicated to Pattini, the goddess of health and chastity, who is also believed by many to have miraculous curative powers.

Take a taxi or auto-rickshaw back to the Fort and your hotel. By now your feet will probably be aching after the long walk. Take a dip in the hotel pool and have a relaxing evening. For dinner, you could try the inexpensive Seafish Restaurant (tel: 2326915) at 15 Sir Chittampalam Gardiner Mawatha, adjoining the Regal cinema, a short distance from the Trans Asia Hotel, or taste Sri Lankan cuisine at the Curry Leaf Restaurant in the cool and romantic setting of the garden of the Colombo Hilton (tel: 2544644).

Right: St Anthony, sacred to various faiths

2. SOUTHERN CITY SIGHTS *(see map, p18–19)*

A full-day's drive touring the south of the city. Shop at Kollupitiya, visit the Sima Malaka temple on Beira Lake, stroll through Viharamahadevi Park, study artefacts at the Colombo National Museum, see the impressive BMICH and the Independence Commemoration Hall.

Begin this tour at the **statue of S.W.R.D. Bandaranaike**, on the left soon after driving past the Presidential Secretariat (*see Itinerary 1, page 22*). The monument, built in honour of the man who was prime minister from 1956 until his assassination in 1959, weighs a hefty 5,080kg (5 tons) and was a gift from the Russians. It stands on its own little hillock overlooking the vast expanse of Galle Face Green and the Indian Ocean. Galle Face Green has lost much of its former glory and attempts are being made to replant grass. At night this is a favourite place for locals to dine in the open-air at makeshift food-vendors' stalls. During the day, it serves as a popular venue for joggers, kite-fliers and hawkers.

Famous Names

The Indian-owned five-star Taj Samudra Hotel (tel: 2446622) lies in its own gardens opposite the green. At the green's southern end, the Galle Face Hotel (tel: 2541010), built in 1864, is a hotel with a guest list that has included many of the 20th century's most famous names; its corridors seem to echo with history (*see page 34*). Under the direction of the company's young chairman, this landmark is gradually being restored. A billiard saloon leads off its broad, front veranda and you can enjoy an inexpensive table d'hôte luncheon while overlooking its lawns. Its Seaspray restaurant (evenings only), by the shore, specialises in seafood.

Further down, on the left of the Galle Road and in front of the Colombo Plaza Hotel (tel: 2437437), you will find the **Crescat** apartment and shopping complex. This is the most upmarket mall in Colombo and a delightful, peaceful place to shop. Its basement incorporates several Asian-food kiosks as well as a supermarket and a laundry. Opposite the mall, you can get useful information on the ground floor of the Sri Lanka Tourist Board

headquarters (78 Stuart Place, Colombo 3; tel: 2437059; email: ctbch@sri.lanka.net). Free maps and brochures are available. Just beyond it is the **Araliyagaha Madiraya** (Temple Trees), the residence of the prime minister. The front entrance is barricaded for security reasons. Virtually opposite are the **American** and **British embassies**, both imposing in their different styles. This area, one of the two main centres for shopping, is known as Kollupitiya; Majestic City at Bambalapitiya is a mile further south.

Turn left at the traffic lights towards Dharmapala Mawatha and you will find a public **market** that sells fresh meat and an array of fresh fish and seafood. Beautifully arranged displays show off the variety of fruit and vegetables grown in Sri Lanka. On the right is the country's first shopping complex, **Liberty Plaza**, which sells wine, clothes and other imports. Further along Dharmapala Mawatha, just before the traffic lights where the road crosses Sir James Peiris Mawatha, a wide range of brassware is laid out on the pavement for sale. Be warned: prices aren't low. Turn left at the lights and, after 180 metres/ yards, the pretty sight of the Buddhist **Sima Malaka Temple,** perched on the serene waters of **Beira Lake**, appears.

The Big Pageant

Park your car and walk to the temple on the wooden platform. Many of the statues inside are from Thailand, and the Sri Lanka antiques have been personally collected by the head monk over the years. Beside the temple a bo tree (*Ficus religiosa*) represents the tree under which the Buddha gained enlightenment. The temple is part of the Gangarama Temple, and in February the area takes on a festive air when the Navam Perahera (procession) parades through the streets, attracting hundreds of

thousands of spectators. Comparable with the Kandy Perahera, it is one of the country's biggest pageants: if you're in Colombo during February, be sure to see it. The neighbouring area is called **Slave Island** after the slaves kept here in Dutch colonial times. They were guarded by crocodiles, and to prevent escape, no boats were allowed on the lake after dark. The Sinhala name Kompanna Vidiya (Company Street) derives from the company of Malay soldiers stationed here during British rule.

Drive down Sir James Peiris Mawatha, turn left at the roundabout and left again to R A de Mel Mawatha, just past the railway station. Drive along the lake, then turn left again at Perahera Mawatha, the picturesque lakeside drive. You are now back at Sir James Peiris Mawatha. Turn right

and after 120 metres (400ft), turn left at Ramanayake Mawatha. Go right at the next junction, Hunupitiya Cross Road, park the car near the *Sunday Times* press and walk the 45metres (150ft) to Dharmapala Mawatha. Here it's worth visiting the arts and crafts shop, **Lakmedura**, which sells brassware, silverware, wood carvings, gems, jewellery, leather products, batiks and lace.

A Miniature Capitol

Return to the car and turn left at Dharmapala Mawatha. On your right is **Viharamahadevi Park**, formerly Victoria Park but renamed in honour of the mother of Sri Lanka's popular national hero, the great Dutugemunu. Turn right at F R Senanayake Mawatha. The entrance to the park on the right is marked by two statues, of the Buddha and Viharamahadevi. The park is beautifully maintained with flowerbeds and green grass amid giant trees. On the left, the **town hall** looks like a miniature version of the Capitol building in Washington DC. Turn left at the end of F.R. Senanayake Mawatha to Dr C.W.W. Kannangara Mawatha. On the left is the white, 100-year-old **Devatagaha Mosque**, a popular spot for beggars in the evenings. Turn round at Lipton's Circus, where tea industry giants Lipton and Brooke Bond once had their offices. A white colonial house at the roundabout serves as the headquarters of Odel Unlimited (tel: 2682712), which sells brand-name clothes and other products at reasonable prices. Down the road (Dharmapala Mawatha again), on the opposite side of the roundabout, the Paradise Road homestore (tel: 2686043) is set in a 'gingerbread' house. You could enjoy a light lunch in the café on its balcony and maybe choose some of the hand-made interior-décor items sold there as unusual souvenirs.

After lunch, drive beyond the roundabout, where C W W Kannangara Mawatha becomes Albert Crescent. On the right is an imposing white building, the **Colombo National Museum** (9am–5pm; closed Fri; tel: 2694767/8) which has a good collection of artefacts. You may wish to spend more time here on another day (*see Itinerary 3*). After the museum, turn left to Albert

Above: Independence Commemoration Hall

Crescent and right at the roundabout to Horton Place, near the petrol kiosk. This residential area boasts fine examples of Sri Lankan-style houses, both old and new. Continue straight past two sets of traffic lights to Castle Street. Take the road to the island's new capital, **Sri Jayewardenepura-Kotte** and turn right at the sign to the **Parliament**. Even from a distance, the new parliament complex, with its Kandy-style architecture, is a beautiful sight, seemingly poised in the middle of the Diyawanna Oya lake. Unfortunately, tight security prevents the public from getting close. Kotte was one of Lanka's ancient capitals and the king was in residence here when the Portuguese, the first Westerners to colonise the island, arrived in 1505.

Showpiece Convention Centre

Return towards Castle Street, but at the roundabout in front of Tickell Road, turn left towards Bauddhaloka Mawatha. On the left is Model Farm Road, which leads to Colombo's 18-hole **golf course**, where visitors can play for a small fee. (Royal Colombo Golf Club, 223 Model Farm Road, Colombo 8; tel: 2695431; fax: 2687592). Drive straight on past Kanatta Cemetery and turn right at the roundabout along Bauddhaloka Mawatha. About 1km (½mile) down this road to the left is the **Bandaranaike Memorial International Conference Hall** (BMICH), the venue of the South Asia Association of Regional Cooperation (SAARC) meetings in 1991 and 1998.

The octagonal building was an official gift from the Chinese government to Sri Lanka in memory of S.W.R.D. Bandaranaike. At a cost of around US$1.5 million, this showpiece convention centre, which can accommodate up to 1,500 people, was completed in 1975. An interesting anecdote lies behind the naming of this building. The name originally proposed, Bandaranaike International Conference Hall, had to be abandoned after it was discreetly brought to the attention of the honouree's widow and then-prime minister Sirimavo Bandaranaike that the acronym BICH was distinctly inappropriate. The word 'Memorial' was consequently added.

To the right of the BMICH is a 1970s replica of the **Aukana Buddha Statue** – the original was carved out of sheer rock sometime around AD400. Further down Bauddhaloka Mawatha you will see the offices of the state-owned television and radio stations. Turn right on Maitland Place, the first street after the BMICH, then left into Independence Square and on to **Independence Commemoration Hall**, where the national independence ceremony was held, amidst great fanfare, on 4 February 1948. The open-sided building was modelled after a Kandy-style royal audience pavilion.

For dinner, go to the Beach Wadiya at No 2 Station Avenue, Wellawatte, Colombo 6 (tel: 2588568), an open-air seafood restaurant. Reservations are

Right: Devatagaha Mosque

highly recommended because it is very popular with the local residents. To get there, travel south along Galle Road from Galle Face Green for about 9km (5 miles) until you see the Savoy Cinema on your right. Turn right to Charlmont Road and continue down the street until the railway line comes into view. The restaurant is on Station Road parallel to the train tracks.

If you would rather eat in central Colombo, you might enjoy a meal in the air-conditioned restaurant – or the friendly bar – of The Cricket Club Café (34 Queens Road, off Duplication Road, Colombo 3; tel: 2501384). This is open daily, even on *poya* national holidays, from 11am to 11pm. Two other excellent restaurants are Thambapani (tel: 2500615) on Duplication Road, for Sri Lankan cuisine, and The Golden Mile (tel: 2733997) in Mount Lavinia, for seafood.

3. COLOMBO NATIONAL MUSEUM *(see map, p18–19)*

Artefacts of ancient Lanka in a British colonial building, including the priceless gem-encrusted Sinhala throne. Half-day tour.

If you don't have time to visit the ancient cities (*see Excursion 6*), an excursion to the **Colombo National Museum** (9am–5pm; closed Fri; tel: 2694767; entrance fee) will provide a taste of the island's rich history and culture. According to the *Mahavamsa*, the monks' chronicle of the island's history, the world's first concept of a museum was recorded between 307BC and 267BC. Drive down Galle Road from Colombo Fort to the Kollupitiya Junction. Turn left to Dharmapala Mawatha and go down to Viharamahadevi Park. Turn right at the roundabout. About 1km (½mile) along Albert Crescent, the museum can be seen on the left. Built in 1887 by the British governor Sir William Gregory, the imposing white building is an excellent example of the architectural style introduced by the British. The museum was built by a Muslim who so pleased his British commissioners that they promised to grant him any reward he chose. The devout man replied that

he would like to be allowed to praise Allah on Fridays. So to this day the museum is closed every Friday to enable its Muslim workers the freedom to worship at the mosque.

The limestone Buddha statue (AD300–500) meditating near the museum entrance was originally found at Toluvila, near Anuradhapura, and is bound to catch your attention. Near the staircase are two 12th-century carvings taken from a rock carving of seven goddesses found in Polonnaruwa, and a carving of the 10th-century Hindu goddess Durga found at Anuradhapura. Though not labelled as such, this is **Gallery 1**. Find a guide to show you around and, if warranted, tip him at your own discretion.

Gallery 2 features clothes worn by aristocrats in days gone by. Look out for the horn combs. The gallery also contains several fine examples of moonstones and guardstones. There are no protective railings to mar your view of the intricate rock carvings. Bronze statues, lamps, carvings of Hindu goddesses and pottery of the 3rd and 4th centuries fill **Gallery 4**. Also displayed are a number of 12th-century Chinese bowls found during excavations at Polonnaruwa. Bronze brassware in **Gallery 6** depicts the cruel deaths of Ehelepola Kumarihamy's children, ordered by the island's last king. There are also some excellent wood and ivory carvings from the 17th and 19th centuries.

Ancient Swords and Guns

A visit to **Gallery 8** is a must, if only to see the collection of royal swords and guns. Note the old Sinhala gun, with intricate carvings on the brass plates, and the sword used by King Buvenekabahu of Yapahuwa. The prize exhibit is a gem-studded throne, made for King Rajasinghe I (1636–87). Even his footstool is studded with gems, and just beside it sits an equally fabulous bejewelled crown. The crown, throne and footstool were appropriated by the British conquerors of Kandy and shipped back to Windsor Castle, where they were kept until their restoration to Sri Lanka in 1934.

The museum's paintings, dating back several centuries, give an insight into a bygone era when the pace of life was more relaxed. There are scenes of Sri Lanka's Aborigines, the Veddahs, hunting with bows and arrows. Look out for the *olas* (palm-leaves) on which Buddhist monks patiently recorded the island's history.

Researchers might want to take advantage of the **Museum Library**, which has more than half a million publications of interest. For children, the fascinating world of puppetry comes alive with the display upstairs. Here you can see the masks used in traditional dances, including the devil dance. The **National Museum of Natural History** (daily 9am–5pm; tel: 2691399) is conveniently situated behind the main museum, and is worth a visit, especially if you're interested in Sri Lanka's wildlife and natural resources.

Left: the National Museum
Above: stone carving of a Hindu goddess in the National Museum

4. GALLE FACE GREEN *(see map, p18–19)*

Politics, vendors and kite-fliers in the centre of Colombo. Spend a few hours watching the many faces of Colombo here.

Drive south on the main artery road from Colombo Fort past the Presidential Secretariat to **Galle Face Green**, which is actually a bit of a misnomer as the area is more brown than green. This, the largest open space in Colombo, is many things to many people: an ideal romantic spot for lovers; a playground for children; an outlet for roadside vendors and their balloons, drinks and ices; an arena for professional types to debate the issues of the day; and a trendy hangout for teenagers.

Observe local colour provided by the likes of the kite seller who displays hundreds of fluttering discs in myriad hues. In the evening, vendors push carts laden with banana chips and fried lentils to the optimum vantage points. At the same time, kiosks complete with tables and chairs are set up on the green for alfresco (and very inexpensive) dining.

Old Charm

The promenade along the sea, stretching for nearly a mile, was built in 1859 by the British governor, Sir Henry Ward, to benefit 'the ladies and children of Colombo'. Due to his foresight, the green retains much of its old charm, with no buildings to mar the beauty of its wide open space. Whether rich or poor, Galle Face Green is accessible to all, and has seen everything from political rallies and musical extravaganzas to horse races.

On one side is **Galle Face Hotel** (established 1864), the oldest grand hotel this side of the Suez, which for many years retained much of its old style without bothering too much about comfort or service. Its former chairman, a noted eccentric, refused to even have a signboard for the hotel, and today his son, Sanjay Gardiner, runs the business. Some of the rooms have been modernised. Signs near the lifts recommend the benefits of walking and advertise discounts for non-smokers. A bust in the foyer of science-fiction novelist Arthur C. Clarke commemorates the time when, as a guest here in 1996, he wrote his sequel, *3001: The Final Episode*. You should experience the charms of the original Galle Face Hotel while you still can – the fine old furniture, the romantic ballroom where dances of yesteryear were held and other memories of a bygone era. With a long drink in hand, sit on the veranda and watch the sunset. Halfway down across the road is the statue of former prime minister S.W.R.D. Bandaranaike, who was assassinated after only three years in office.

Above: the Kiteman of Galle Face Green

5. KELANIYA RAJAMAHA VIHARE *(see map, p18–19)*

A half-day tour to the Kelaniya Temple where, according to legend, the Buddha is reputed to have sat when he preached for peace.

Drive east from Colombo Fort and turn right after crossing the Kelaniya Bridge. Turn right soon after Peliyagoda to the road which leads to the **Kelaniya Rajamaha Vihare** temple, a distance of about 11km (7 miles). The temple's history goes back more than 2,500 years. It is believed that the Buddha visited Kelaniya and preached from a bejewelled chair to warring factions on the futility of fighting. The original dagoba was said to have enshrined the chair but was later destroyed by Indian invaders. Restored in the 13th century, the Kelaniya Temple again suffered at the hands of invaders in the 16th century, this time the Portuguese.

Wrath of the Gods

Be sure to see two important statues here: the reclining Buddha and the Buddha in a meditative pose. And you could spend hours gazing at the extraordinary frescoes that depict the life of the Buddha and important events in the island's history. One fresco tells the story of King Kelanitissa, who boiled a Buddhist monk in oil because he wrongly suspected the monk of trying to pass a love letter to the queen. The angry gods raised tidal waves and the king was told that the only way to appease them was to sacrifice his daughter Viharamahedevi (whose statue can be seen in Viharamahadevi Park opposite the town hall) to the sea. The king did as he was told, the waters calmed and Viharamahedevi, swept out to sea on a gold-encrusted boat, landed at Kirinda near a minor kingdom in the south of the island.

There the handsome Prince Kavantissa had been told by a soothsayer that he should marry only if a girl were to arrive by sea in a golden boat. He married the princess immediately and their first son, Dutugemunu, became a legendary hero who defeated the Tamil King Elara in an epic battle and went on to unite the country under one monarch for the first time.

The Kelaniya Temple is a hive of colourful, frenetic activity at the time of the January full moon, when hundreds of elephants and dancers parade through the streets during the Duruthu Perahera festival.

Right: fresco in the Kelaniya temple

6. DEHIWALA ZOO *(see map, p37)*

Both adults and chilren will enjoy a few hours at this zoo. Visit in the afternoon to catch the performance of dancing elephants.

The **Dehiwala Zoo** (daily, 8.30am–6pm; tel: 2712751; entrance fee) is one of the largest zoos in Southeast Asia and its sprawling grounds are host to an impressive collection of birds, reptiles and other animals. To get there, drive 9km (6 miles) south along Galle Road from Colombo city centre. Take a left turn at Anagarika Dharmapala Mawatha, Dehiwala, and then follow the signposts.

The zoo pioneered the policy of placing animals in an artificial habitat, rather than simply displaying them in cages, as happens at so many zoos around the world. Here lions, bears, tigers, rhinos, giraffes and gorillas all benefit from a relatively high degree of freedom. In the **Reptile House** you will find a rare albino cobra and an enormous python. Watch out for the little tortoises that ride piggyback on ferocious crocodiles. The zoo also has an excellent collection of primates. Don't miss the 500 varieties of marine life at the **Mini Medura** (aquarium), which was designed with children in mind – youngsters dart around the exhibit like the fish in the tanks. The **Nocturnal House** allows visitors to see night creatures such as owls and lemurs in their natural habitat.

Elephant Circus

Sri Lankans love elephants and are accustomed to living and working with them, so it's hardly surprising that the highlight of the zoo is the elephant circus, which takes place every afternoon at 4.30pm.

The enormous pachyderms perform all sorts of unlikely antics, such as standing on their heads, wiggling their backs to music, playing a mouth organ, hopping on one foot, sitting on stools and standing on their hind legs. Many people take the view that the spectacle of performing elephants is old-fashioned, as well as being cruel and degrading to the animals. But if you do stay around to see the show, be sure to catch the death-defying moment when an elephant places a foot on the stomach of the mahout (trainer). Another popular trick involves the elephant lifting the mahout by the head with its mouth.

The end of the elephant show signals a mass exodus from the zoo, so it's a good idea to get your bearings in advance. That way you can quickly make your way to the exit and then drive or take a taxi back to Colombo, without getting caught in the crush.

Above: too big for his seat

7. MOUNT LAVINIA *(see map, p37)*

Yearning for a sandy beach and the crash of waves, but too lazy to drive too far out? Head for Mount Lavinia, only 13km (8 miles) from Colombo.

Mount Lavinia is one of the loveliest beach areas close to any metropolis in the world, and it is a mere 13km (8 miles) from the heart of Colombo. To get there, drive south along Galle Road from Colombo Fort and turn right to Hotel Road, about 1km (½ mile) past the Mount Lavinia cemetery.

The **Mount Lavinia Hotel** remains the focal point of Mount Lavinia, though there are newer hotels, such as the Berjaya Mount Royal Beach Hotel, which opened in the 1970s. The hotel was built in 1810 as a residence for a British governor. Legend has it that the governor fell in love with a *rodiya* (outcaste) girl who worked for him. When the governor was leaving, he asked her what she would like as a gift. To his surprise, she asked for official permission to wear a cloth to cover her breasts – a mark of status normally denied to the outcaste.

Bathing huts on the beach can be hired for the day. When hunger pangs gnaw, head for the Curry Clipper at Mount Lavinia Hotel or adjourn to one of the seafood restaurants on the beach. The Golden Mile on College Avenue is recommended.

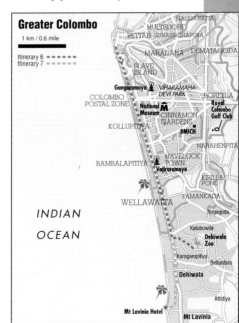

Above: a haul of exotic fish

Excursions

1. KANDY, THE HILL CAPITAL *(see maps, p40 & 42)*

Journey through pineapple country, a cashew village and the world's only elephant orphanage; climb Utuwankanda and Kadugannawa for the spectacular views and cool breezes of Kandy's hill country; visit the sacred Temple of the Tooth. Stay overnight or drive through the campus of Peradeniya University before returning to Colombo.

The road to Kandy is an exciting one that races through lowlands before climbing steep passes into what was, in the early 19th century, the citadel of power for Sri Lankan kings. The road on which you will be driving, the A1, is in fairly good condition – it was the first to be built in the country by the British. Depart at about 6.30am, as there is a lot to see. If you fancy fresh pineapples for breakfast, you can buy them on the way. On leaving Colombo, turn right at the Kelani Bridge onto the Kandy Road. About 26km (16 miles) from Colombo, near **Yakkala**, rows of pineapple stalls line the roadside. The best and sweetest pineapples in the country are grown right here. Take a break to feast on the freshly plucked fruit.

Roasted Cashews

You will notice the pleasant smell of roasted cashew nuts near milestone 29 at **Cadjugama** (Village of Cashews), where women sell the nuts to passing motorists from roadside stalls. What began as an attempt by bus drivers' wives to supplement their income soon developed into a village tradition. There are more street vendors at the next milestone at **Wewaldeniya** (Grove of Cane), where you can buy cane chairs, cane-crafted elephants, bamboo lamps and bamboo baskets.

If there is time, take a trip to **Kota Vihare**, an archaeological site and birthplace of one of Sri Lanka's greatest kings, Parakramabahu the Great (1153–1186). To get there, turn right off the main road at Nelundeniya junction and continue via Dedigama. One of the most fascinating objects on view at the nearby **Archaeological Museum** (9am–4pm; closed Tues) is a brass elephant lamp found within the dagoba. The lamp has an oil tray in which a brass elephant hangs from intricately carved chains. When the wicks are lit and the oil falls below a certain level, the elephant exudes more oil to keep the lamp burning. The design is based on a hydraulic principle, and the visitor can only

Left: a modern Kandyan chief in the Perahera procession
Right: elephant on parade

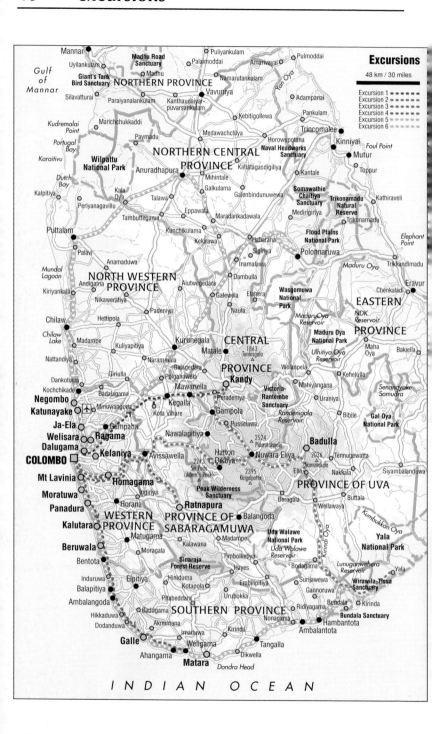

stand back in amazement at the technology of a lamp made 800 years ago.

Return to the main road, and a little way past milestone 45, you will find the **Ambanpitiya Tea Factory**. The factory welcomes visitors, and in the course of a 20-minute tour you can see how tea is prepared, from the time the fresh green leaves arrive from the plantations to the crushing, fermentation and drying stages. It is then ready to be packed for the tea auctions in Colombo. Packets are available for sale and you might well want to sample a cup of freshly brewed tea with snacks sold on site.

After a satisfying cuppa, race on to Karandupona. Past Kegalla, a signpost marks the left turn to the **Pinnawela Elephant Orphanage**. Be warned: if you decide to visit this attraction en route to Colombo from Kandy, there is no sign marking this turn. The state-run orphanage is about a 5-km (3-mile) drive past some small, privately operated elephant sideshows. Don't stop, but go for the real thing. There are more than 50 elephants in the orphanage, from calves of only a few weeks to magnificent, fully mature specimens. This, the only such sanctuary in the world, primarily cares for calves abandoned or lost in the wild. It trains its elephants, which are eventually given to temples or sold to foreign zoos. The orphanage is one of the very few places in the world that has been able to breed elephants in captivity successfully.

It is a good idea to visit the orphanage during feeding or bathing times. The very young are fed from bottles, much like human babies. Feeding times are at 9.15am, 1.15pm and 5pm; bathing times from 10am–noon and from 2–4pm. The bathing takes place at the end of the road opposite the entrance to the orphanage compound. You buy your tickets at the main en-

trance and then walk down the road to the river. At a given command, the older elephants guide the younger ones towards the river. They playfully squirt water on themselves and each other, and then lie down, hind legs first, immersing themselves completely except for their trunks. The ma-

houts climb on top of the larger elephants and help scrub them down. A photo of a mahout taking a nap on the back of a bathing elephant makes a fine souvenir of this orphanage. Perch yourself on the riverside rocks and enjoy the entertainment. You can purchase drinks at sites overlooking the bath scene, or take lunch at the Ceylon Hotels Corporation restaurant in the grounds. There is a branch of Hatton National Bank opposite the orphanage entrance and, behind it, the Elephant View Hotel where, for a small charge, you can see the skeleton of a giant elephant.

Sri Lanka's Robin Hood

The **Nilwala Spice and Herbal Garden** (2 Pinnawala Road) is about 460 metres (1,500ft) down the drive back to the Kandy road. Take a guided tour to learn how spices and herbs grow, and to become acquainted with their medicinal properties. Return to the main road and turn left to resume the journey to Kandy. A solitary hill, **Utuwankanda**, indicates the place where Saradiel, the figure known as Sri Lanka's Robin Hood, lived in the 19th century. Saradiel terrorised the rich and gave the booty to the poor. He was eventually captured and sentenced to death by the British rulers.

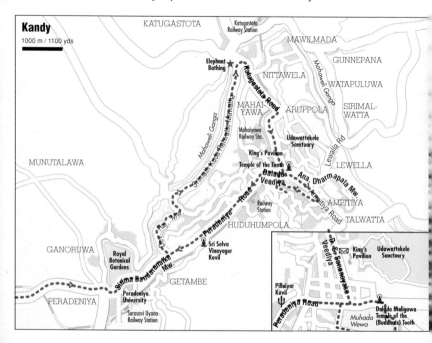

The **Kadugannawa** climb starts near milestone 59 – a sign appropriately announces a 'Thirst Aid Station'. A rubber hose connected to a natural hill spring is conveniently placed for drivers desperate to fill vehicle radiators with water before the steep climb. The scenery from here is breathtaking, with terraced paddy fields, sheer drops and lush green vegetation. **Bible Rock**, so named because it resembles an open bible, comes into view on the right. Fruit stalls selling avocado and the pungent *durian* are a common sight on your way from Kadugannawa to **Peradeniya**. Cross the Peradeniya Bridge and stop for lunch at the Peradeniya Rest House (tel: 08 388299) opposite the gateway to the Peradeniya Gardens.

Once you have satisfied your hunger and quenched your thirst, turn right out of the rest house and continue on the main road to Kandy for about 1km (½mile). One can take the direct road to Kandy or detour by turning left into Srimath Ratwatte Mawatha. This road takes you along the banks of the Mahaweli, the island's longest river, which emerges at Katugastota. Here, turn right and drive 3km (2 miles) towards Kandy, which is situated 500 metres (1,600ft) above sea level.

The Prettiest City

Kandy, nestling among green hills with the lake as its centrepiece, is perhaps the prettiest of all the country's cities. This was the seat of the last king of Sri Lanka until the British captured him in 1815. Drive first along the lake on Lake Drive

and go up **Rajapihilla Mawatha** to appreciate the full splendour of Kandy below. To the right, the Temple of the Tooth, complete with recently constructed golden roof, looks resplendent. Some say the king kept his mistresses, or miscreants, on the island in the middle of the lake.

Return to Lake Drive and proceed to the **Temple of the Tooth**, which is visible in the distance. The tooth of the Buddha, enshrined in the octagonal temple, was brought to Sri Lanka in the 4th century from India, hidden in the hair of a princess. The tooth is one of Sri Lanka's most venerated objects; it has become not only the island's most prized possession, but its very seal of sovereignty. A replica of the tooth is ceremonially paraded through the streets every year. This custom first began over 1,500 years ago, and the procession is now the oldest such regular historical pageant in the world. The procession, the **Esala Perahera**, is held in July–August and features hundreds of colourfully-clad elephants and thousands of whirling dancers parading through the streets for 10 consecutive nights.

Get to the temple by early afternoon. Security checks at the entrance, at the archway to the fenced park in front of the temple, are taken very seriously.

Above Left: one of many fine carvings at the Temple of the Tooth
Above: a paddy field on the outskirts of Kandy

A notice prohibits 'short trousers, mini skirts and sleeveless jackets, blouses or gowns'. There is an admission fee.

Leave your shoes at a stand in front of the temple. You will see hundreds of fish in the surrounding moat and, near the staircase, fine carvings of elephants. If you are not lucky enough to be here during the Esala Perahera celebrations, try to conjure up the image of an elephant climbing up the steps to receive the replica of the tooth. The tooth, secreted amidst seven dagoba-shaped caskets, is richly decorated with jewels and precious stones presented by royalty over the centuries. Unfortunately the tooth relic itself is not on display.

During Esala Perahera, bare-torsoed drummers in white headdresses and sarongs beat a steady tattoo, while thousands of worshippers offer flowers. The tall wooden pillars are typical of Kandyan architecture. To the left is the museum where the remains of the magnificent tusker, Raja, can be seen. This elephant, who carried the temple's treasure in the Perehera, is officially a national treasure. A stamp has been issued in its honour.

When you leave the temple (don't forget to collect your shoes), walk about 60 metres (200ft) to the statue of **Madduma Bandara**, the boy hero of 1814. The legend goes as follows: when the king of Kandy heard of a plot by one of his ministers to murder him, he ordered the minister's family to be killed. When his elder brother flinched as he faced the executioner, the nine-year-old Bandara said, 'Fear not, dear brother. I will show you how to confront death.' With that, he walked boldly up to the executioner to meet his fate.

Arts and Crafts

Drive on for about 1km (½mile) to the **Kandyan Arts and Crafts Association** showroom near the Red Cross. Founded in the early 1880s to protect and encourage genuine Kandyan arts and crafts, the association was the first of its kind in the country. Here are excellent examples of Dumbara hemp mats (often used as wall hangings), lacquerware and fine jewellery. Return to the Kandy-Peradeniya Road and stop at the **Royal Botanical Gardens** (entrance fee, plus parking charge), once the pleasure gardens of the queen. Its 60ha (150 acres) are filled with tropical plants of every description. Turn right soon after entering the gardens to see the beautifully arranged flowers. The orchid house has some rare species while the plant house contains leafy house varieties. Other attractions include the giant banyan trees, the coco-de-mer (double coconut but given its name because sailors once thought it grew in the sea) from the Seychelles, the giant bamboo and an aromatic spice garden with carefully labelled trees.

Above: coconuts for sale

It's time to call it a day. Drive through the beautiful **Peradeniya University Campus** before taking the road towards the capital. Plan to leave at 4.30pm to reach the city by about 7.30pm. Alternatively you may wish to spend the night in one of Kandy's hotels (prior reservation is recommended). The Queen's Hotel (Dalada Veediya, Kandy; tel: 0812 233290; fax: 0812 232079) is a 19th-century hostelry that was once the haunt of British planters and aristocracy, and is well-placed opposite the Temple of the Tooth. The place retains the atmosphere of colonial days, especially its Pub Royale at the end of the next-door arcade, where local delicacies like egg hoppers and beef curry are available in the evenings. There is another pub, called The Pub, above a bakery at 36 Dalada Veediya, about 92 metres (300ft) away. You can sit on the balcony and watch the activity in the main street below, or dine inexpensively in the attached restaurant.

A more exclusive retreat is the simple but elegant Regent Lodge (172 Riverdale Road, Kandy; tel: 0812 232032; fax: 0812 233213; e-mail: regentlg@sri.lanka.net). Overlooking the Mahaweli River this moderately priced hotel, 10 minutes' drive from the city centre, has seven double rooms and is set into a verdant hillside.

Traditional Dancing and Drumming

If you are staying in Kandy for the night, you will have an opportunity to see a Kandyan dancing show. At the Kandyan Arts Association Hall in Avanhala (behind the Temple of the Tooth), an hour-long performance begins at 6pm every evening (tickets cost Rs250 at the time of writing). This fascinating display of traditional dancing and drumming is worth making an effort to see.

If you have enough time to spare, you could drive for some 45 minutes from Kandy along the Katugastota Road and towards Wattegama to the Hunas Falls Hotel at Elkaduwa (tel: 0812 470041). This is a luxury resort (complete with miniature golf course and swimming pool) located in the midst of a tea and spice estate set beside a lake and rising above a waterfall.

Another lovely place to stay, about 13km (8 miles) from Kandy, is the Hotel Tree of Life at Yahalatenna on the Kandy-Kurunegala Road, This 26-ha (65-acre) property includes chalets, cottages and an Ayurvedic clinic and herbal treatment centre (tel: 0812 499777; fax: 0812 499711; e-mail: tolhotel@sltnet.lk). You might extend this Kandy trip with a visit to the hill station of Nuwara Eliya (*see Excursion 2*).

Right: relaxing by Kandy Lake

2. THE COOL HILLS OF NUWARA ELIYA *(see map, p40)*

For those who love the hills area and want to enjoy its salubrious climate, an extension of the Kandy visit to Nuwara Eliya is recommended. A full-day with the option of an overnight stay.

Nuwara Eliya is a haunting reminder of the period of British rule, not least as a result of its setting and colonial-style houses. In 1818, four years after the Kandyan kingdom had been ceded to the British, a hunting party led by Dr John Davy, brother of the scientist Sir Humphrey Davy, chanced upon Nuwara Eliya. In 1828, the governor, Sir Edward Barnes, turned the highland site into a health resort and sanatorium for British officials who wanted to escape the oppressive heat of the lowlands.

In 1847, Sir Samuel Baker, the explorer and discoverer of the source of the White Nile, decided to build a home in Nuwara Eliya. Using elephant-drawn carts, Baker transported all that was necessary for an English country town, including a blacksmith's forge, Hereford cows and even a bailiff. The Elizabethan-style mansion that was originally built for the governor is today the Grand Hotel of Nuwara Eliya. Fashionable circles in Colombo like to converge here in April, when temperatures begin to rise in the commercial capital. The green hills, the cool weather, the beautiful lake and parks all combine to make Nuwara Eliya the most pleasant hill resort on the island.

To get there from Kandy, turn left past the Peradeniya Bridge towards Gampola. Follow the winding road and signposts to Nuwara Eliya. The air here becomes significantly cooler so remember to take a jacket or sweater to keep you warm on the drive up through verdant tea plantations and waterfalls. It is only 69km (43 miles) from Kandy, but the climb is steep so the drive can take nearly two hours, or longer if it's foggy.

In Nuwara Eliya, drive through the town, passing the park on the left, on Badulla Road for a short distance and turn right at Grand Hotel Road. The

Above: Ella, the entrance to the hill country from the south

100-year-old, 150-room **Grand Hotel** (tel: 052 222 2881/fax: 052 222 2265) has a lovely lawn with brightly coloured flowerbeds. If you spent the day in Kandy and arrived late, the air will be nippy. Check into a large room with a fireplace and take a warm bath. If there's time, you might want to take a stroll into town – a five-minute walk from the hotel along the road adjacent to the golf course and down Lawson Road. A popular haunt in Lawson Road is the Beer Shop where the locally brewed Lion lager is sold on draught. To treat yourself to a table d'hôte dinner the way the British planters would have enjoyed it – with waiters in white gloves and gentlemen in ties – book a table at the nearby Hill Club (tel: 052 222 2653).

Jaw Rock

The following morning, after a buffet breakfast, drive out of the hotel, turn right and travel about 10km (6 miles) on the Badulla Road to **Hakgala Gardens** (entrance fee, plus parking charge). Hakgala means 'the jaw rock': according to local legend, the rocky mountain was brought here by Hanuman, the monkey god featured in the Hindu epic, *Ramayana*. Rama wanted Hanu-

man to go to the Himalayas and bring a medicinal plant which grew there. Hanuman reached the mountains but forgot the name of the plant. So he brought a part of the Himalayas with him, hoping that the required plant would be included. About 1.5km (1 mile) before the Hakgala Gardens on the right is another place associated with the *Ramayana*, the Sita temple where the kidnapped Sita, Rama's wife, was held captive.

Drive through some beautiful gardens and stop near the rose garden. About 100 different varieties are planted here. There are exotic species, too, named after personalities such as Elizabeth Taylor and Theodore Roosevelt. Stroll through orchid houses, foliage houses and on to a lovely area with quaint bridges, rushing streams and what looks like every type of fern in the world. Most trees are labelled. A colony of monkeys that live near the summer house often perform antics for visitors in the hope of being fed. Return to Nuwara Eliya, past vegetable gardens on the hillsides and colourful stalls selling the produce by the road.

Visit the **Hill Club**, which is more than 100 years old and a two-minute walk to the rear of the hotel. Only in 1967, long after the end of the colonial period, were Sri Lankans allowed to join a club that had been the exclusive domain of British tea-planters. Some of the members' complaints and comments – recorded in a book kept in the hall – make fascinating reading. A Mr P.P. Blackmore wrote in September 1902: 'Would suggest use of Bromo toilet

Above: local transport takes its time

paper in the closets in place of the present stuff which is like cardboard'. The club is very British in many ways, with hunting trophies of trout and deer displayed prominently. Original encyclopedias line the library's shelves and the antique billiard table is a collector's item.

A short distance from the Hill Club along Grand Hotel Road is the 36-ha (90-acre) **Nuwara Eliya Golf Club**, established in 1889. The 18-hole course is one of the best, and prettiest, in the entire continent. It is also said to be the only golf course in the world where all the holes can either be seen from the clubhouse or followed by car. It's worth checking out the monument to the notorious elephant hunter Major Rogers, in the little cemetery behind the clubhouse. Rogers is reputed to have killed some 1,500 elephants over the 10 years he spent hunting them. He died (not trampled by an elephant, which would certainly have been poetic justice) when struck by lightning, which folklore associates with elephants. In the intervening years, Rogers's grave is said to have been struck twice by lightning.

The Highest Mountain

To get to the daily fair, return to the club entrance and follow the road to town via the Windsor Hotel. The fair is full of colourful stalls that sell everything from clothes, shoes, plastic goods and toys to raw vegetables and cooked food. Take a walk past the souvenir shops in town to **Lake Gregory**, the lovely artificial lake which makes the town so pretty. The lake's banks are sometimes lined with fortune-hunters hoping to find gems in the water.

Standing on the shores of the lake, you should be able to see Mount Pidurutalagala. With Nuwara Eliya resting at its foot, **Pidurutalagala** is, at 2,524 metres (8,281ft), the highest mountain in Sri Lanka. At Nuwara Eliya you are already 1,889 metres (6,197ft) high, so climbing Pidurutalagala should not pose any problems, but don't go too close to the state-owned television tower at the summit, which is guarded by soldiers who are under orders to shoot all trespassers. The view from the top is spectacular, with Nuwara Eliya in particular looking like a fairy-tale village. Continue to the **racecourse** on Badulla Road. The track is only a shadow of its former glory but the strawberry-and-carnation plantation at the centre is interesting. From the front of the Grand Hotel, take the road to Kandapola to a unique luxury hotel, **The Tea Factory** (tel: 052 222 9600/fax: 052 222 9606), set in the shell of an abandoned tea factory amidst a green tea plantation.

Have a quick lunch at the hotel and drive back to Colombo. En route, via Ginigathena, look across a spectacular vista on the right for **St Clair's Falls**. You might want to visit the **St Clair's Tea Centre**, run by Melsna

Above: schoolboys wait for a bus

Tea, for a cup of tea and a slice or two of chocolate cake. At **Kitulgala**, 96km (60 miles) from Colombo, the 14-room **Kitulgala Resthouse** (tel: 03622 87528) has a magnificent view of the Kelani River and the surrounding countryside. The walls feature photographs of the filming of David Lean's Oscar-winning epic movie *The Bridge on the River Kwai*, which was filmed at Kitulgala. Continue the journey, turning right to Colombo or left to Ratnapura (*see Excursion 3*) at Avissawella. Should you choose to extend your stay by several days it is possible to drive from Nuwara Eliya down to the Yala National Park (*see Excursion 5*) and back to Colombo via the south coast to Galle and along the west coast via Bentota.

From Nuwara Eliya, take the road to Hakgala and drive on to Welimada where you turn right and continue southwards to the tea-plantation town of **Bandarawela**. Not as popular with foreign visitors as Nuwara Eliya, Bandarawela nevertheless has a good hotel and lots of scenic attractions. A night at the **Bandarawela Hotel** (tel: 057 222 2501) with its tea-planter club atmosphere of long lounge with chintzy armchairs and rooms with old-fashioned, brass-knobbed beds, is memorable. The hotel is peaceful (it was a sanatorium in the 1930s) and the food good. If you want to meet the locals, head for the bar at the back of the building, where they tend to congregate.

Pink Quartz and Buffalo Curd

On the next day continue the drive along the Badulla road to **Ella**. The view from the Ella rest house of Ella Gap tops most you will see in Sri Lanka. Rice and curry for lunch is a good choice here. Near the rest house is a cave where, in one of the most stirring episodes in the *Ramayana* epic, the demon Rawana is supposed to have kept Sita, wife of Rama. Continue on the road down the gap from Ella towards Wellawaya to see the spectacular Rawana Ella Falls. Young boys will offer pieces of pink quartz for sale when you stop to gaze at the falls; they make nice paperweights. Be sure to enjoy the lushness of the scenery because, after Wellawaya the road, the A2, drifts through dry landscape to Tissamaharama.

Buffalo skulls by roadside signs indicate sales of buffalo curd. This is a rich, wholesome form of yoghurt made with buffalo's milk. It is sold in clay pots and is often eaten with palm treacle. From Tissamaharama continue south to the coast and turn left just before Kirinda towards the Yala National Park. Stay at the Yala Village Hotel (*see Excursion 5*) for a comfortable version of jungle life. Crocodiles sunbathe on the rocks by the restaurant and elephants wade across the lagoon.

Right: St Clair's Falls

3. RATNAPURA, THE CITY OF GEMS *(see map, p40)*

A day-long excursion to the City of Gems. Learn how gems are mined and cut before visiting the Pothgul Vihare temple, built in the 1st century BC.

Ratnapura is only 100km (60 miles) from Colombo and found fame as Sinbad's legendary Valley of Diamonds in the tale *1001 Arabian Nights*. Solomon reputedly used gems from Ratnapura to entice Sheba. Travellers have long waxed eloquent about the island's rich treasures, which lay buried under rocks and earth. The Venetian explorer Marco Polo wrote about the King of Lanka wearing a priceless, flawless ruby a span in length.

If coming from Colombo, leave by 7am, after a good breakfast. From the Colombo Fort area take Galle Road for about 6km (4 miles) to Dickmans Road, then turn left just before Saint Paul's Milagiriya Church. Turn right into Havelock Road, which at Kirilapone becomes High Level Road. Continue towards Avissawella, 45km (28 miles) from Colombo, and take the right fork towards Ratnapura. If travelling from Nuwara Eliya, the journey takes about five hours. Remember to turn left at Avissawella.

Rubber Country

This is scenic rubber country and the road runs through seemingly endless plantations. Stop at a plantation to see containers, often empty coconut shells, secured to the tree trunks to collect the milky white latex that drips down from the incision. At **Eheliyagoda**, the gateway to gem-land, new prosperity is evident in the shops and houses. Past the Kuruwita signpost, the **tea estates** begin. The two leaves and a single bud plucked from each tea bush throughout the year is transformed into one of the island's leading exports. Just outside Ratnapura, you come to an unmarked fork. Both roads lead to Ratnapura, but the broader road in front is better and is one of the few stretches in Sri Lanka where your car can safely pick up speed.

When you arrive, head straight for the **Ratnapura Rest House** (tel: 04522 22299) about 1km (½ mile) past the bus stop on Hill Road. Turn left and follow the signs. Order lunch for 1pm, which gives you time to browse around Ratnapura. The Ratnapura Rest House gem shop has a fine selec-

tion of stones. Drive back to the bus stop, turn left and travel about 1.5 km (1 mile) to **Council Avenue,** where gem dealers sell natural, uncut stones.

Turn left and travel about 1km (½ mile) on Council Avenue to Pothgul Vihare Road. Be warned that there are no signs on this road to guide you to Pothgul Vihare, so after about 5km (3 miles), turn right where you see the sign to Rajasilagama to visit a **gem mine**. Make sure that you get there before the workers finish for the day at 1pm. Park your car and climb up to the sound of a motor pumping out water. At the mine, you will see pits that 2–9 metres (6–30ft) in depth, their sides supported by logs or planks arranged in a criss-cross fashion. Men dressed in loincloths work hard to bring the alluvial soil from the gem pit up to the surface. Nearby, the soil is washed in a large wicker basket. As the lighter sand gets washed off, the heavier stones fall to the bottom. The man brings up the basket, and after a short prayer, begins to sort through the stones. There is eager expectation in the eyes of all watching: some end up millionaires; most remain paupers.

Pothgul Vihare Temple

After all that glitter, it is time to reflect on life's simpler virtues. The steep climb up 450 steps to the **Pothgul Vihare** temple, originally built by King

Valagambahu (89–77BC), begins here. There is no drinking water at the summit, so remember to take your own bottle. You will certainly need a drink by the time you reach the temple at the top. There you can take in the spectacular scenery of the surrounding hills.

A massive rock forms the temple roof. There are two caves with old paintings and a statue of a reclining Buddha. Unusually, it is possible to walk round to the back of the statue and have a good look. Outside is a sculpture of an open-mouthed devil and, on top of the rock, a figure ready to jump between the devil's jaws. This depicts one of the 550 lives of the Buddha, in which he sacrifices himself by jumping into the mouth of a devil. Ascend and return to the Ratnapura Rest House, to freshen up after the hot and sweaty climb. After lunch, head for the **Saman Devale**, about 3km (2 miles) along the Ratnapura–Horana Road. This was built in the 13th century but the original buildings were destroyed by the Portuguese in the 17th century.

Return to Ratnapura and travel 1.5km (1 mile) on the Badulla Road to the sign which directs you to Ehelapola Mawatha in the village of **Batugedera**. The fascinating **Gemmological Museum** (daily 8.30am–5.30pm, tel: 04522 22398; free), owned by A.G.B. Amarasinghe, includes exhibits of different types of natural rocks from all over the world as well as local gems. Visitors are often intrigued to see gem-cutters demonstrate their techniques of cutting precious stones and polishing them on machines. Take time for some refreshments in the museum cafeteria before heading back to Colombo.

Left: a gem-studded armlet
Above: tapping rubber

4. SOUTHERN COAST ESCAPADE *(see map, p40)*

Drive through a region of remarkable diversity. Shop for local wares; see 'toddy tappers'; visit a mask factory; observe the ocean's marvels in a glass-bottom boat; see stilt fishermen; or simply laze the day away on a sandy cove. Although this tour can be done in a day, you will probably want to take it easy and linger a few days at one of the many beach resorts.

The most popular beach resorts are on the southern coast. Despite extensive destruction caused by the 2004 tsunami, the tourism sector has been quick to rebuild. The beaches are sandier than those on the west coast and the eastern coast remains less accessible. The south of Sri Lanka is a prosperous area, studded with beautiful bays, hills, wildlife and plantations of tea, rubber and coconut. A day is not enough to see everything, but you could try.

Getting to the south is easy. Take the Galle Road, which hugs the coast past Mount Lavinia (*see Itinerary 7*). Little of the sea is actually visible until Moratuwa, about 21km (13 miles) from Colombo. At **Wadduwa**, little stalls sell reed baskets, coir and straw mats with eye-catching designs and bamboo lampshades. Piles of mangosteens, a succulent, creamy-fleshed fruit, are sold throughout the year at **Kalutara**, 45km (28 miles) out of Colombo. Mangosteens are plentiful throughout the island, but Kalutara is reputed to have the best. But be careful not to get the reddish-brown juice of the mangosteen shell on your clothes as the sap stains indelibly.

Kalutara Dagoba

Drive across the two bridges. Were it not for the convenient island in the middle, this would have been one very long bridge across the **Kalu Ganga**. On

the other side is the white **dagoba of Kalutara**. Every Buddhist driver drops a coin into the till outside the temple to ensure a safe journey. The dagoba is unusual in that it is hollow inside with a smaller stupa in the centre of the hollow space. Look at the walls lined with paintings depicting the lives of the Buddha. As the dagoba is hollow and dome-shaped, words spoken by those standing on the other side can be heard quite clearly. There are magnificent views of the bridges and ocean beyond.

Just past Kalutara, to the right, lies the pleasant Kani Lanka Resort and Spa (tel: 03422 26537) with its lovely gardens. The hotel offers watersports on the lagoon of the Kalu Ganga.

Pass Katukurunda, an abandoned British airstrip now used for motorcycle and car races. Just beyond milestone 31, there is a breathtaking view of the sea, beach and coconut trees. The island's full beauty unfolds

Left: Unawatuna Beach

from here onwards. The ropes connecting the coconut trees are for high-wire toddy tappers who risk life and limb to tap the flower of the coconut tree for its sap, which, when fermented, is known as toddy, a cheap alcoholic beverage. Toddy is big business in Sri Lanka. The sap is also used to produce treacle and *jaggery*, a kind of brown sugar.

Drive through **Beruwala** and, at milestone 35, Alutgama – a Muslim fishing town full of mosques – to the beautiful holiday resort of **Bentota**, at milestone 40. The waters at Bentota beach tend to be calm except during the monsoon season. October through April are the best months for swimming. Stop at the stunning boutique hotel **Taru Villas** (tel: 03422 75618), where the food and the rooms are exquisite. Alternatively, there is the 135-room **Bentota Beach Hotel** (tel: 03422 75176), which is built on the site of an old Portuguese fort, with a large garden and natural-rock swimming pool. Near the sandy beach, with rockpools fringed by coconut trees, you might catch sight of the hotel's elephant mascot. Non-residents can get a ride, though the mahout expects at least Rs100. The Club Intersport (tel: 03422 75178) next to the Bentota Beach is part of the hotel and is open to non-residents; it's recommended for watersports enthusiasts, who can have fun either at sea or on Bentota River.

Ayurvedic and Holistic Rejuvenation

A plush new hotel, Taj Exotica (tel: 03422 75650; fax: 03422 75160) has been built on a bluff overlooking the length of the beach but it is rather too formal for the holiday atmosphere of this beachside village. There are several good, inexpensive small hotels and guesthouses in Bentota. You might stay in the riverside pavilions of **Aida's Ayurveda and Holistic Health Resort** (192 Galle Road, Bentota; tel: 03422 75397; fax: 03422 75275) and be rejuvenated by a herbal diet, flower baths and natural-oil treatments or, at Aida's adjoining licensed restaurant, by seafood or steak.

You might see fishermen hauling in their daily catch. Chanting 'Odi, helai, helai laam', to the resonant screech of seagulls, the fishermen tug at their nets. No one will object if you give a hand. Once the nets are in, the slippery heaps of fish are quickly gathered and divided up.

The beautiful 2-ha (5-acre) garden **Brief** (daily 9am–5pm; entrance fee) at Kalawila was once owned by the late Bevis Bawa. Turn right at Alutgama along the Matugama Road just before reaching Bentota. After 5km (3 miles), past Dharga Town, turn left at Ambagaha Handiya (Mango Tree Junction) and turn right at the mosque after 1km (½ mile). Follow the signs 'To Brief' and turn right at the sign 'Short cut to Brief'. This road is better than the normal route, but remember to take a sharp right at the sign 'To Gardens'. A few yards up the hill, drive through the imposing gates and ring the bell

Above: Kalutara dagoba

at the house. The gardens alone are worth the entry fee. Bevis Bawa, who, at 1.8 metres (6ft), was once Sri Lanka's tallest man, left his entire estate to his staff, who valiantly try to maintain his standards. After visiting the gardens, ask the caretaker, Mr de Silva, to show you the house and its antiques. He might even allow you to see Bevis's 2.1 metres (7ft) bed.

Bevis's brother, Geoffrey, Sri Lanka's foremost architect, also has a garden in Bentota called *Lunuganga* which, alas, is not open to visitors. Robin Maughan, in his book about the garden, describes *Lunuganga* as 'paradise, a shangri-la, a glimpse of *nirvana*'. The sprawling house in the middle of this oasis houses much fine antique furniture, several of Bevis' paintings and works by George Keyt and the painter, Donald Friend.

Proceed along the coast to **Kosgoda**, where, despite the impact of the tsunami, some turtles have returned to hatcheries. Signs of the human cost of the tragedy become more obvious the further south you go. While some stretches of coastline appear untouched, others are home to rows of temporary housing. Locals, though, remain desperately keen for tourists to visit, and a warm welcome can be expected. Stop at **Ambalangoda**, which is famous for its masks and puppets. Just before milestone 53 and the turn-off on the left is the **Ariyapala mask factory**. Mainly used in devil dancing, which is known for its grotesque movements, the colourful masks produced here have large, protruding eyes and big teeth.

Drive through Ambalangoda town to **Hikkaduwa**, where an unchecked tourism boom led to an indiscriminate rash of hotels on the beach. There are several diverting bars and cafés here and, despite its surge in popularity, it is a pleasant place to break the drive for refreshment. The town is popular with backpackers in search of an inexpensive and lively place to stay.

Dutch Fort

Continue your journey to **Galle**, 116km (72 miles) from Colombo, where The **Lighthouse**, a new 5-star hotel (tel: 09122 23744; fax: 09122 24021), is worth visiting. It is about 3km (2 miles) before Galle and there is a panoromic view from the bar. Sadly, the town remains synonymous with the events of December 26, 2004, as television pictures of the raging waters engulfing it were beamed around the world. Reconstruction is well underway, though, and the main landmark in Galle, the beautifully preserved 36-ha (90-acre) **Dutch fort**, largely escaped damage – its gateway's 14m- (45ft-) thick walls having been built to withstand enemy cannonballs.

Above the gateway is the coat of arms of Great Britain and Ireland. Inside, carved on stone, is the monogram of the Dutch East Indies Company. More than 300 years old, it is marked by two lions on either side and a cock perched on a rock as the crest. A walk along the ramparts reveals an ingenious sewerage system designed by the Dutch, which is cleared when the tide is high. Within the fort are several important churches, including the oldest Protestant church in the country, the **Groote Kerk**. Visit the luxurious

Above: coins for sale at the Dutch fort
Right: stilt fishermen

new **Amagalla** hotel (tel: 09122 33388), occupying a 300-year-old Dutch colonial building. In its previous guise as the New Oriental, it was the oldest hotel on the island and survived from the days of sailing ships, when Galle was the main port. High ceilings, large easy chairs and a lovely garden at the rear give it great character. Competition, though, comes from the chic **Galle Fort Hotel** (09122 32870) nearby. The **mansion** museum (tel: 09122 23214) on **Leyn Baan Street** in the fort is also a must see.

A hotel worth visiting outside the fort is **Hotel Closenberg** (tel/fax: 09122 32241), which was the residence of Captain Bailey, the agent of the P&O Company, in the mid-19th century. Today, it has 20 rooms and a magnificent view. Proceed along the Galle-Matara road and turn right to **Unawatuna Beach**, which is one of the finest on the island. The sand stretches out lazily in a secluded bay and there is no shortage of space. Return to the main road and travel to **Koggala**. Here, an abandoned airstrip on the left became the island's third Investment Promotion Zone in 1991.

Weligama

During the last leg of the journey, visit **Weligama**, 145km (90 miles) along the Galle-Matara road. It's a very pleasant drive and the little sandy bays with coconut trees growing on the seashore have adorned tourist advertisements for Sri Lanka for years. A community of **stilt fishermen** lives between Ahangama and Weligama. The fishermen sit patiently with the tools of their trade – sticks driven into the seabed.

After taking refreshments and listening to the roar of the sea at the **Weligama Bay Inn** (tel: 04122 50299), an island not far from the inn will catch your eye. This is **Galduwa** (Rock Island). Known to some as Yakinige Dowa, 'She-Devil's Island', this garden isle was purchased by Count de Mauny, a French expatriate, in the 1930s. The count converted the island into an exquisite garden, encircling a nine-room, octagonal, jewel-like mansion decorated with eclectic handicrafts. The mansion is partially hidden by the shrubs but, if the tide is low, you can easily wade out to it across the little jetty. But be warned that security here is somewhat forbidding.

On your return trip to Colombo, stop at a convenient spot to see the sun set over the sea. With so many beaches to choose from, it is highly unlikely that you will want to return to Colombo straight away.

5. YALA NATIONAL PARK *(see map, p40)*

Sri Lanka is elephant country but the population is fast dwindling. Spend a night in Yala National Park in search of this magnificent mammal, and also the elusive leopard. This excursion can be taken from Colombo or as an extension of Excursion 4 (*see page 52*).

Established in 1899, **Yala National Park** in the south is recommended for the wide variety of species to be seen in the 1,295 sq km (500 sq mile) sanctuary. Hire a jeep with driver locally at Tissamaharama. Book your accommodation at **Yala Village Hotel** (tel: 0115 373305; fax: 0115 373304; www.srilanka.com). If starting your journey from Colombo, plan to leave at about 7am and head south on the Colombo-Galle-Matara road. Continue along the coast for 195km (122 miles) to **Tangalla**. Have lunch at the **Tangalla Bay Hotel** (tel/fax: 04722 40346) on the right just before the town. Swimming is not recommended, but the view is beautiful from this hotel, which was modelled after a ship.

From Tangalla, continue for 43km (27 miles) to Hambantota. The lush low vegetation gives way to thorny plants and small shrubs, typical vegetation of the dry zone. Drive on for 26km (16 miles) on the main road along the coast, which gradually turns inland towards **Tissamaharama**. Turn right into town and stop to arrange a jeep for the excursion to the Yala National Park. Singha Lanka Tours at the Tissamaharma Resthouse (tel: 04722 37299) will help get you a vehicle. To reach the hotel, take the lonely Kirinda road with the beautiful Tissa Maha Seya Dagoba on your left. The hotel is set amid shrub and protected from the sea by sand dunes. Check in, have a cool, refreshing drink and wait for the jeep to arrive.

Entry hours to the park are from 5.45am to 3.30pm, although you are allowed to stay till 6.30pm. In addition to the entrance fee, you have to pay the tracker assigned by the park. The trackers are experienced in the ways

Above: contemplating a dip

of the jungle and usually prove to be very interesting companions. There is a small museum near the entrance which is worth seeing, but leave it for the next day if you run out of time. The tracker will show you the places to find wildlife, including buffaloes, crocodiles, sambars, monkeys, flying squirrels and a wide variety of birds that migrate from India and as far afield as Europe. These spots are usually near water holes, where the animals come to drink in the evening and early morning.

On December 26, 2004, rangers reported seeing buffalo running inland moments before the wave struck. Soon the animals of Yala became the stuff of legend as it was reported around the world that they may have sensed the tsunami was coming. In truth, the reserve itself sustained little damage. There are patches where the sea broke through, but few of the big mammals were in danger. Either way, they seem none the worse for the experience. Yala is still teeming with wildlife. It is a magical place.

Spotting a Leopard

It's a wonderful sight to see herds of deer, sometimes 60- to 100-strong, grazing or just gazing at visitors. Painted storks, herons, ibis and egrets abound. But the greatest thrill is the sight of wild elephants and leopards. The elephant found in Sri Lanka belongs to the same sub-species as that found throughout Asia. These huge creatures move majestically and are seldom bothered about visitors, except when they feel threatened. Leopards are rare at Yala – spotting one would be the the highlight of an adventure in the park. A persistent tracker sometimes finds one, usually seen playing like an overgrown cat on the road. Keep a look out for these handsome animals which, although widespread throughout the island, are not often seen as they are nocturnal.

Return to the hotel at dusk, wash off the dust and retire. Don't forget that the jeep will be back early in the morning. After another tour of the park, return to the hotel at about 9am for breakfast and perhaps a leisurely stroll down to the beach, where you can visit the colony of migratory fishermen who have pitched their huts here.

Leave for Colombo, returning to the Tissamaharama-Kirinda Road where you turn right. At **Kirinda** there is a lovely view of the southern coast from a temple atop a rock. This is the spot where Viharamahadevi, the mother of the Sinhala hero Dutugemunu, is said to have landed. She had been sent out to sea on a boat as a sacrifice by her father, King Kelanitissa of Kelaniya, to placate angry gods.

Continue to Colombo along the same road and at Mawella, look out for the blowhole ('hummanaya' in Sinhala) that shoots a jet of water high up into the air. Take a break for some lunch at the Dikwella or Dondra, which is the southernmost point on Sri Lanka, before turning and heading north once again.

Right: tree with natural cavity

6. RUINED CITIES OF THE NORTH
(see maps, p40, 60 & 64)

A two-day excursion into Sri Lanka's past. Visit the historic sites of Dambulla, Polonnaruwa, Sigiriya and Anuradhapura.

An overnight trip to the island's ancient historical sites – or what Sri Lankans call the ruined cities – is a worthwhile expedition. More than 2,500 years old, some of the sites are better preserved than others. A two-day trip encompasses Dambulla, Polonnaruwa, Sigiriya and Anuradhapura. The engineering skill of these early Sri Lankans is something to behold. Only at Sigiriya would you

find water gardens built atop solid rock 1,500 years ago. A recent attempt to divert the island's longest river, the Mahaweli, had overseas experts studying land contours and water flow for months, with the help of computers and science. Concluding that a major diversion should be made at Minipe, they found evidence of a similar attempt made 1,000 years ago.

There is a fee for the permit to visit all four sites; individual permits can also be purchased at the sites. Children aged between 8 and 12 pay half. The tickets, including a permit to take photographs, can be obtained either at the sites or in Colombo from the central Cultural Fund, 212/1 Bauddhaloka Mawatha, Colombo 7 (tel: 2500733; fax: 2500731; email: gen_ccf@sri.lanka.net).

Depart at 6am to reach Dambulla by 10am, as the rock caves are closed 11am–2pm. Take the Colombo-Kandy Road and turn left to Kurunegala at the signpost. Take the Dambulla Road from Kurunegala, 93km (58 miles) from Colombo. At Dambulla, 150km (93 miles) from Colombo, turn right at Kandy Road. The rock caves are on the right after Dambulla Rest House.

Dambulla Cave Temple

The **Dambulla Cave Temple**, the most impressive of Sri Lanka's many cave temples, is a must. King Valagambahu fled here from Anuradhapura in the 1st century BC when Indian Tamils captured the capital. After regaining his capital, the king built a temple in the caves where he had hidden. But it was King Nissankamalla of Polonnaruwa who gilded the interior of the caves, later known as Rangiri (Gold Rock) Dambulla. There are five caves and the 107-m (350-ft) climb to the temple is well worth the effort. The very first cave is the smallest but it has a 14m (45ft) reclining Buddha carved out of solid rock. In the temple grounds you will find the largest gold Buddha statue in the world, a recent construction.

Some of the decaying frescoes depicting the lives of the Buddha are being restored. A statue of King Valagambahu, stands watch over the images

Above: Kurunegala
Right: inside the Dambulla Cave Temple

of Buddha (of which there are 100) and Hindu gods. Freshen up and have drinks at the **Dambulla Rest House** (tel: 06622 84799), run by the Ceylon Hotels Corporation (Travel Bureau, 411 Galle Road, Colombo 4; tel: 2503497; fax: 2503504.) Return to the Colombo-Anuradhapura-Kandy road junction and turn right to Habarana and then right again towards Polonnaruwa. There are no signposts at Habarana to indicate where to turn so look out for the police station at the junction. The Habarana-Polonnaruwa stretch is one of the loneliest in this area and it is not unusual to see wild animals, including deer, monkeys and iguanas. The road is generally good but watch out for jagged edges and unmarked bends.

Polonnaruwa was at its zenith of power and glory in the 11th century but the capital city lasted only 200 years. Its most illustrious king, Parakramabahu I (1153–86), presided over the only era when rice was exported and Sri Lankans first ventured overseas. About 1.5km (1 mile) before the town, the ruins suddenly come into view on the left. As lunchtime approaches, continue for another 1.5km (1 mile) and turn right towards the Polonnaruwa Rest House. The **Parakrama Samudra** (Ocean of Parakrama), a vast reservoir of water covering 2,430ha (6,000 acres), lies before you. The amazing King Parakramabahu, who built the reservoir, proclaimed that not one drop of water should escape into the ocean without it being of some service to man.

A Vital Reservoir

Today, as it was in ancient times, the reservoir is the lifeblood of the region. It provides precious irrigation water for some 7,365ha (18,200 acres) of paddy land. Along the bund, about 2km (1½ miles) on, is **The Village**, Polonnaruwa, formerly Hotel Amalian Nivas (tel: 02722 22405), where you can order lunch. While your meal is being prepared, drive 1km (½ mile) along the road to a statue carved on a rock. Depending on the source, this is either King Parakramabahu or Agastaya, an Indian religious teacher.

Return to have lunch and then drive up to the ancient ruins. Tickets are checked at a security post or can be purchased here. King Parakramabahu's **Royal Palace** is to the right. Of the original seven floors, only three remain.

A staircase leads nowhere, but its former grandeur can be imagined. The brick walls have big holes for the ceiling's giant beams. Ancient books tell of a lift to transport palace workers to the top floors.

In front of the Royal Palace is the administrative building and audience hall, which were restored by the British. Some fine specimens of elephant carvings have been preserved, but even the best craftsmen make mistakes – no prizes for spotting the five-legged elephant near one of the entrances. Notice the interesting change in the moonstones, the semi-circular works of art found near entrances to important buildings. In contrast with the Anuradhapura moonstones that you will see tomorrow, the ox has gone from the design, a change attributed to the Hindu influence which considers the ox sacred.

Royal Bath

Nearby is a beautiful tree with a natural cavity, ideal for children to hide in. Just below are the remains of the walls and the royal bath, **Kumara Pokuna**, a large, exquisite stepped bath of cut stone. Underground stone conduits feed it with water from the Parakrama Samudra. However, only two of the original five crocodile spouts for water are still intact.

Drive back to the security post and turn right down the gravel path. As the reign in Polonnaruwa was brief, most of the important ruins are confined to a smaller area than in Anuradhapura. About 1.5km (1 mile) down this road is a solitary post on the left. This is the **Sangadhikaranayaka** (The Court of the Monks), where Buddhist monks who misbehaved were put on trial by their peers. They were then defrocked and banished to a village called Hiraluwa to become farmers. To this day, a monk who has left the order is called a

Polonnaruwa

1.6 km / 1 mile

Quadrangle
Buddha Image
Chapter House
Hatadage
Atadage
Hindu Shrines
Sathmahal Prasadaya
Gal Potha
Lata Mandapaya
Bo Tree Shrine
Vatadage
Boddhisattva
Thuparamaya

Tivanka Pilgrimage (Image House)

Demala Maha Seya

Gal Vihare (Uttararama)

Naipena Devale
Kiri Vehera
Alahana Pirivena
Shiva Devale
Lankatilaka
Gopata Pabbata
Buddha Sima Pasada
Rankot Vihare
Nissanka Pavilion
Menik Vehera
Pokuna
Archaeological Museum
Gate
Vishnu Devale
Shiva Devale
Shiva Devale
Summer Palace
Pabulu Vehera (Parakramabahu)
Sangadhikaranayaka
Quadrangle
Dipuyyana (Nissanka Mallas Palace)
Shiva Devale
Citatel
Audience Hall
Ticket Office
Kumara Pokuna (Royal Bath)
Vejayanta Prasada (Royal Palace)
Ranketha
Parakrama Samudra
Market
OLD TOWN
Nippon
Chinese Rest House
Neela Tourist Lodge
Devi Tourist Home
The Village
Statue of Parakramabahu/ Agastaya
Seruwa
Pothgul Vehera
National Holiday Resort
NEW TOWN
Sri Lanka Inn

hiraluwa by the Sinhalese. Try a coconut at the nearby refreshment stand. After the juice has been drunk, the vendor will split the coconut open. Eat part of the flesh and throw the remainder to the monkeys. Their agility is incredible as they jump to catch what you offer.

A number of ruins are concentrated in the **Quadrangle**. Climb the steps to the **Sathmahal Prasadaya** (seven-storey dagoba) on the right. Its former seven floors show a distinct Burmese influence – Parakramabahu established meaningful contacts with that country. Next is the massive 9-metre (30-ft) long **Gal Potha** (Rock Book), one of the longest and heaviest of its kind in the world. The enormous slab of stone is 1.5 metres (5ft) wide and over 60cm (2ft) thick. The rock is inscribed with the great achievements of Parakramabahu's successor and nephew, Nissankamalla who, in a hurry to outdo his uncle, indulged in an orgy of monument- and temple-building. A footnote reveals that the Rock Book was brought from Mihintale, over 100km (60 miles) away. The 25-ton book was believed to have been transported to its present site on wooden rollers tugged by elephants.

Nearby is the **Hatadage**, where the tooth of the Buddha was once believed to have been housed. Built by King Nissankamalla, its columns are adorned by erotic carvings. To prevent destruction by Tamil Hindu adventurers, the king had bulls carved at the entrance, but his precaution failed to work. Next is the **Atadage**, built by King Parakramabahu's predecessor, King Vijayabahu, which at one time also housed the Buddha's tooth. The altar opposite the Buddha image was believed to be the position where King Nissankamalla sat listening to Buddhist discourses.

The wonders of Thuparamaya

The **Thuparamaya** temple is the only building here with a roof, and it contains nine statues of the Buddha. One is broken but others, made of quartz and containing mica, glisten magically. Light a candle and the wonders of Thuparamaya are revealed. One statue is believed to have had gems embedded as eyes. These emitted strange rays when sunlight streaked in from specially constructed angled crevices.

The **Vatadage** is a beautiful, circular relic house built by King Parakramabahu. It is probably the oldest building in Polonnaruwa, preceding the establishment of the capital by several centuries. Do not be deceived by the inscription

Above: among the ruins of the Royal Palace. **Right:** Sathmahal Prasadaya

made by King Nissankamalla claiming he built it. Politicians taking credit for the achievements of others is an old trait in Sri Lanka. The four entrances lead to four Buddha statues and a central dagoba. Again, one of the statues is broken, but the grandeur of the place remains intact, despite the lack of a roof. The main entrance has a well-preserved rock moonstone flanked by two guardstones. Beyond the Vatadage is the **Shiva Temple**, where the *yoni* and *lingum*, symbols of fertility, are worshipped by Hindu women seeking blessings for conception. Remove your shoes and headgear before entering temples and dagobas.

Continue your journey in the car. To the left, you will see the **Rankot Vihare** (Golden Pinnacle), a dagoba standing 40 metres (125ft) high with a circumference of 170 metres (550ft). The remains of the **Alahana Pirivena** (university) and the **royal burial grounds** are located nearby. Drive on to a car park with some souvenir stalls and alight to visit the well-preserved **Kiri Vehera** (Milk Dagoba) and the image house, **Lankatilaka**, which has 17 me-

tre- (56ft-) thick walls and a headless statue of the standing Buddha.

Cross the road and walk to the **Gal Vihare** (Rock Temple), where a quartet of statues of the Buddha, carved out of sheer rock, comprise some of the finest existing legacies of the work of 11th-century craftsmen. The disciple Ananda stands beside the Buddha, his arms folded and one leg bent in the *Tivanka* posture. The most detailed and impressive statue is the 13-metre (43-ft) reclin-

Above: locals crowd the Vatadage
Left: Gal Vihare's seated Buddha

ing Buddha. Check out the slight depression in the pillow beneath his head, and the marks on the soles of his feet. The seated Buddha in deep meditation is under an arch and, beside him, in a cave, is a smaller Buddha with his attendants. On the left of the cave are the frescoes, amazingly still in their original colours, that once adorned the walls.

There is more to see in Polonnaruwa, but by now it will be about time to leave. Return to the car and the Habarana Road. About 5km (3 miles) from Polonnaruwa, stop by **Jayanthipura** at the **Pubudu Lace Centre**, an open building on the left. Beautiful lace souvenirs, including table mats, table-cloths, curtains and pillowcases, as well as batik dresses, are sold here.

Sounds of the Jungle

Spend the night at **The Village** (tel: 06622 70046) in **Habarana**, a lovely property with a swimming pool, gardens and rooms in separate chalets. If there aren't any rooms available at The Village, try the adjoining up-market **The Lodge** (tel: 06622 70011) or **Hotel Kandalama** (tel: 06622 84100; website: www.aitkenspencehotels.lk) in Kandalama off the Dambulla Road, a gaunt hotel set against the Kandalama rock with a breathtaking view of the

Kandalama Tank. Hearing the sounds of the jungle and the grunts of wild animals at night is one of the pleasures of these hotels. Enjoy gazing at the stars in a clear sky and reflect on what you have seen during the day.

Next morning, leave at about 7am for Sigiriya to avoid climbing in the midday heat. Turn right at The Village gate and after about 26km (16 miles), just past milestone 98, turn left at the Sigiriya sign. The entrance fee is US$10 (2004 rates) if you do not already have a ticket. On the approach road, watch out for monkeys in the old fortifications on the right.

Sigiriya palace, built by King Kassapa (AD447–495), was fashioned after Mount Kailas, home of the gods. Sri Lanka is promoting it as the eighth Wonder of the World. In search of wealth, Kassapa killed his father and then chased his brother, Moggalana, to India. Sigiriya palace was impregnable, but Kassapa met his doom on the plains. Hearing that his brother had raised an army and was coming to wage war, Kassapa set out with his army to surprise them. At the height of the battle, the king's elephant, sensing a hidden swamp before it, momentarily turned aside. Kassapa's army, fearing their leader had turned in retreat, broke in confusion. Left defenceless, the king decided to take his own life.

Kassapa's palace is built on top of a huge rock, rising about 200m (650ft), and the only access is through the mouth of a lion whose likeness was once

Above: Sigiriya, the Lion Rock monolith

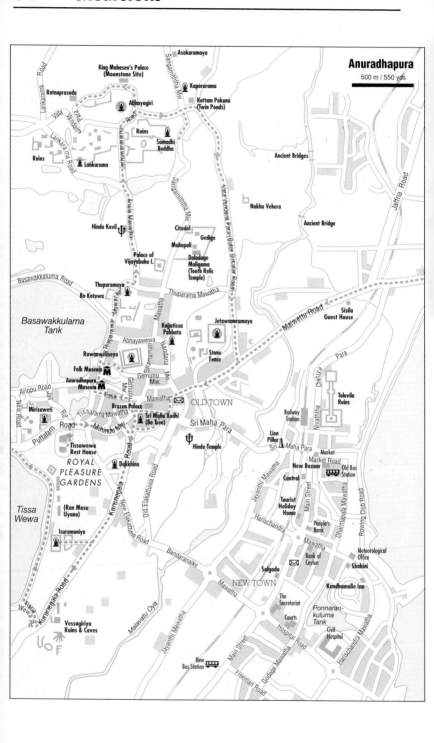

Anuradhapura

500 m / 550 yds

Asokaramaya

King Mahasen's Palace
(Moonstone Site)

Kapararama

Ratnaprasada

Abhayagiri

Kuttam Pokuna
(Twin Ponds)

Ruins

Samadhi
Buddha

Ruins

Lankarama

Ancient Bridges

Nakha Vehera

Ancient Bridge

Hindu Kovil

Citadel

Gedige

Mahapali

Palace of
Vijayabahu I.

Daladage
Maligama
(Tooth Relic
Temple)

Basawakkatuma Road

Thuparamaya

Thuparama Mawatha

Bo Kotuwa

Sisila
Guest House

Basawakkulama
Tank

Jetawanaramaya

Kujjatissa
Pabbata

Abhayaweva

Malwetta Road

Nandana

Ruwanweliseya

Stone
Fence

Folk Museum

Gemunu
Mw.

Anuradhapura
Museum

Toluvila
Ruins

Arippu Road

Tissa

OLD TOWN

Railway
Station

Mihindu Mw.

Brazen Palace

Mawatha

Mirisaweti

Sri Maha Bodhi
(Bo Tree)

Sri Maha Para

Lion
Pillar

Puttalam
Road

Tissawewa
Rest House

Hindu Temple

Market

Market Road

New Bazaar

Old Bus
Station

ROYAL
PLEASURE
GARDENS

Dakkhina

Central

Tissa
Wewa

(Ran Masu
Uyana)

Tourist
Holiday
Home

Isurumuniya

Harischandra

People's
Bank

Mawatha

Bank of
Ceylon

Meteorological
Office

Salgada

Shahini

NEW TOWN

Kondhamalie Inn

The
Secretariat

Ponnaran-
kuluma
Tank

Vessagiriya
Ruins & Caves

Courts

Civil
Hospital

Hospital Road

New
Bus Station

Freeman Road

carved halfway up the monolith – hence the name Sigiriya (**Lion Rock**). A moat filled with crocodiles once guarded the entrance. UNESCO is now restoring the pleasure gardens at the foot of the rock.

A brick stairway and spiral staircase lead you to the **Art Gallery**, which once had 500 frescoes of heavenly maidens. Today, only about 18 of these frescoes remain but, unfortunately, you can't even see all of these because one section of the gallery is closed to the public. What can be seen is certainly delightful. Voluptuous, naked maidens holding baskets of flowers float among clouds. No one knows whether the seductive beauties – painted in tempera in brilliant colours on the rock wall – were meant to be goddesses, Kassapa's concubines or dancers, but the sophisticated use of colour and form over 1,500 years ago expresses an amazing level of artistry.

Climb past the **Mirror Wall**, which once doubled the frescoes with their reflections. Try to ignore the old and new graffiti. Halfway up, there is a refreshment stall where prices are triple the normal rate. This is not as unreasonable as it seems – drinks have to be carried a great distance to the stall. The final climb to the top is via a crude staircase cut into the rock, which at least has a handrail. Called **Lion Terrace**, it is bound on three sides by a low parapet, with a sheer cliff cutting down from the fourth (south) side. One can only imagine the intimidating military advantage the city must have had when the enemy had to enter this path through the jaws of the menacing beast. You have to climb through two clawed paws to reach the steep stairwell. This climb is not for the fainthearted, but for those who do venture forth, the view from the terrace is breathtaking. Unfortunately, only the foundations are visible, but the deep (27 metres by 21 metres/88ft by 68ft) pool cut into the rock makes one wonder at the size of the workforce needed to create such an imposing fortress.

Craftsmen At Work

Go back to the main road and stop for a while at the **New Gamini Ebony Workshop** to see wood craftsmen at work. Jewellery boxes inlaid with porcupine quills sell for about Rs1,250. Take a short break at Sigiriya Village, a 10-ha (25-acre) resort that really is like a village, with clusters of cottages in a shady park and an open-sided restaurant with delicious meals served on trestle tables made from local timber (tel: 06622 31803).

Above: fresco of a heavenly maiden
Right: Buddhist offerings

Once refreshed, take the Sigiriya-Anuradhapura Road. On reaching the Old Town in Anuradhapura, stop at the Tissawewa Rest House (tel: 02522 22299; fax: 02522 23265) located in a park that was formerly part of the Royal Pleasure Gardens. Try the local speciality, rice and curry, for lunch here while watching monkeys gambolling around this attractive retreat.

There are any number of things to see at Sri Lanka's first capital, founded by King Pandukhabaya in 380BC. In contrast to Polonnaruwa's brief and uncomplicated history, **Anuradhapura** remained the island's capital for more than 1,400 years, before pressure from the Tamils of south India finally left no option but to move it eastwards.

In 247BC, Mahinda, the son of Emperor Ashoka of India, helped Pandukhabaya's grandson, King Devanampiyatissa, to become a Buddhist. This led to a flurry of building activity, in particular the construction of temples and dagobas, as people wanted to follow the Buddhist tradition of performing meritorious acts. As Anuradhapura is in the dry zone, and the storage of water in reservoirs is vital for agriculture, these people developed a tremendous knowledge of construction, water conservation and management.

Sacred Bo Tree

Drive to the **Sri Maha Bodhi**, the Sacred Bo Tree, which grew from a sapling of the original bo tree of Bodhgaya in India, under which the Buddha gained enlightenment. This is the oldest historically documented tree in the world, brought to Sri Lanka by Sangamitta, the daughter of Emperor Ashoka in the 3rd century BC. Encircled by a gold-plated railing, it stands amidst other younger trees on a special platform, a *bodhigara*. Most of the island's bo trees have been nurtured from Maha Bodhi's seeds.

Watering the bo tree is considered an act of devotion by Buddhists so you might find any number of pilgrims, pots of water in hand, helping to nourish the plant. It is prohibited to pluck the leaves but there is nothing to prevent you from taking a fallen leaf as a souvenir. Near the bo tree is the **Brazen Palace**, which once had a bronze roof, nine floors and housed 1,000 monks, of whom the most senior occupied the top floor. How did he get to his quarters? By an elevator, according to historical records, though no other details are available. Only about 1,600 stone pillars now remain of what once must have been an impressive building.

Above: entrance to the Sacred Bo Tree site
Right: trilingual signpost to a once impressive palace

Drive along the road between the tree and the palace to the **Anuradhapura Museum** (9am–5pm; closed Thurs, Fri and public holidays; tel: 02522-22589; entrance fee), which has numerous fine carvings from the Anuradhapura era and a model of the Thuparama Vatadage, complete with wooden roof. At the entrance to the right is a statue of the man who devoted his life to the discoveries of an ancient civilisation – Dr Senarath Paranavitarana. Among the interesting exhibits note the female figures on the guardstones; an indication that King Kassapa employed women as guards. There are agricultural implements, coins, pots and even impressions of a dog's paw and a man's toe on some bricks. Take note also of the museum's remarkable umbrella-like roof.

Drive towards the north and see the **Ruwanweliseya**, a dagoba constructed by King Dutugemunu (161–137BC), the hero of the Sinhala race. It was the king who liberated Anuradhapura from the Tamil yoke by vanquishing King Elara; but he was so horrified by the wanton destruction of life that he decided to devote the rest of his own life to building dagobas. Ruwanweliseya, which stands more than 150-metre (500-ft) high, including a 90-metre (300ft) dome, is his best-known construction, and regarded as probably the greatest of Anuradhapura's dagobas. Unfortunately Dutugemunu did not live to see the completion of the dagoba – the *Mahawamsa* describes how white cloth was draped around the semi-finished building for the dying monarch to see his greatest work. The wall has a frieze of elephants, and the limestone statue is believed to represent King Dutugemunu.

The Buddha's Collarbone

Turn left and drive north to the **Thuparamaya**, which is not only the oldest dagoba on the island, but is believed to contain the right collarbone of the Buddha. The dagoba was built by King Devanampiyatissa and stands just over 20 metres (60ft) high. Constructed entirely out of earth in the 3rd century BC, this dagoba has, like a work in progress, been improved upon and embellished by a succession of rulers. Its present 'bell' shape is the result of major restoration work carried out in 1862. Drive along Anula Mawatha, towards the **Abhayagiri Dagoba**, which was constructed by King Valagambahu (89–77BC). Today this structure stands 74 metres (243ft) high, although according to historical records, when restored by King Parakramabahu, it was even more impressive as it rose to a total height of 100 metres (328ft).

Turn left to **King Mahasen's Palace**. Among the ruins, at the threshold of the Queen's Pavilion, you can observe

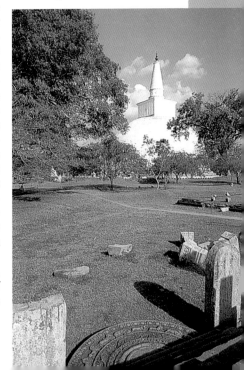

Right: outside the Ruwanweliseya

the very finest moonstone in Anuradhapura, cut on rock. A little way further up the road is the **Ratnaprasada**, built in the 8th century, and which has two of the best-preserved guardstones of the Anuradhapura era. The *naga* (snake)

king sits under a *makara* (dragon) arch, with a flowerpot and lotus stalk – two symbols Sri Lankans associate with abundance and prosperity. Return to the Abhayagiri Dagoba, turn right at the crossroads and drive straight down to the **Samadhi Buddha**, an excellent example of sculpture from the 4th century.

Return to the crossroads, turn right and visit the rectangular twin ponds, the **Kuttam Pokuna**. According to records, the water supply was piped underground from 6km (4 miles) away and entered the smaller pond through the mouth of the *makara*, Sri Lanka's equivalent of the dragon. The **five-headed cobra**, can be seen near the *makara*. Drive along the outer circular road (Vata Vandana) to the **Jetawanaramaya**, the world's largest dagoba. Built by King Mahasen (AD273–303), it was originally over 122 metres (400ft) high, with a diameter of 110 metres (370ft). Occupying some 3.2ha (8 acres) of land, it is just a little smaller than the Great Pyramid of Egypt.

Limestone Lovers

The final visit is to **Isurumuniya** rock temple. To reach it, drive on the road south until you see the Brazen Palace on your right. Turn left soon after passing the bo tree and go south towards the **Tissawewa Tank**. It is ascribed to King Devanampiyatissa who, in the 3rd century BC, made it Anuradhapura's chief source of water. Isurumuniya, built in the 3rd century BC as part of a monastic complex called Issiramana, is on the right.

Here stands the famous 4th-century limestone carving of the Isurumuniya lovers, a man and a woman immortalised in song. The woman lifts a warning finger but the man carries on regardless. Some say the figures represent Dutugemunu's son, Saliya, and a low-caste maiden whom he loved. As you climb towards the cave containing a statue of the reclining Buddha

cut from rock, note the sculpture of two elephants splashing water. Nearby, a carving in high relief features a man, probably a prince, with a horse looking over his shoulder.

To return to Colombo, take the A12 out of Anuradhapura heading westwards to **Puttalam**. The town, located beside a lagoon, has the lethargic, laconic atmosphere of a forgotten frontier. Turn left onto the A3 here for the drive down the coast for 130km (82 miles) if you go straight through to Colombo.

In **Chilaw**, the next major town, a billowing sea breeze stirs up waters of the lagoon and ruffles the sails of the fishing boats moored there. This colourful, albeit somewhat sleepy, town will probably come as something of a relief after the consistently drab and arid scenery of the road. There is a pleasant beachside rest house if you fancy some refreshments before continuing the drive southwards to Negombo. The **Munneswaram Temple** (on the A3), complete with renowned Tamil inscriptions, is a popular destination for pilgrims, and you might see some devotees walking there from Chilaw, 1km (½ mile) away.

Picturesque Negombo

Negombo owes its status as a favourite resort town to its proximity (about 20 minutes drive) to Bandaranaike International Airport at Katunayake. It is a pleasant place to stay, neither as up-market as Bentota, nor as down-market as Hikkaduwa, its beach resort counterparts south of Colombo. The settlement was founded by Arab traders but today this fishing village is populated mostly by Roman Catholics, a legacy of its Portuguese connection, which ended in 1640 when the town was captured by the Dutch. At sunset, the red sails of the local fishing boats on the beach form a beautiful sight in this most picturesque of resorts.

There are several good hotels with moderate rates as well as numerous guesthouses where you should be able to find a room without advance notice. The leading hotel hereabouts is **The Royal Oceanic** (tel: 03122 79000; fax: 03122 79999), situated at Ethukala, just before you reach Negombo town. Advance reservations can be made through Jetwing Hotels (tel: 345700; email: jethot@srilanka.net). If you decide to stay the night, you can while away the evening by visiting some of the local bars before dinner at your hotel or guesthouse. On the following day you can enjoy a leisurely cruise on the backwater canals before taking the short drive of 40km (25 miles) back to Colombo.

Above Left: the legendary lovers of Isurumuniya
Left: Tissawewa Tank. **Above:** local children walk tall

Leisure
Activities

SHOPPING

Gems, batiks and handicrafts are among the recommended articles to purchase in Sri Lanka, although a wide variety of imported goods are also available. Though shopping may not be as cheap as in Hong Kong, the number of Indians who come to Colombo just to shop suggests that prices are still lower than in that country. The main shopping areas are in the **Fort** and **Pettah** districts, though gem shops are ubiquitous throughout Colombo, particularly along **Galle Road** and **R A de Mel Mawatha**.

With the establishment of shopping complexes in Colombo, notably the **Liberty Plaza** in Kollupitiya, **Majestic City** in Bambalapitiya and the upmarket Crescat Shopping complex adjoining the Colombo Plaza Hotel, there now exist commercial hubs where the visitor can find an eclectic selection of nicely displayed and attractive items. There are also specialist stores dealing in clothes and home-décor articles. These match the best overseas stores, with remarkably low prices.

Gems

An immense assortment of gems can be found on the island. It is difficult to give sample prices because each stone is unique and its cost depends on a number of factors, such as colour, size and shape.

Blue sapphires are the best buy in Sri Lanka. The stones are usually not price-marked, and the customer is expected to-bargain with the vendor. Unless something really takes your fancy and you feel you must have it, the best thing to do is look around and compare prices before making a purchase. Gem merchants are accustomed to paying a commission to people who have brought them customers (which could include the taxi driver who delivers you to the jeweller, even if it's at your own request), go shopping without a local escort and you should get a lower price.

Star sapphires and star rubies produce a gleam with six rays when light falls on them and are beautiful when set as rings and pendants. Alexandrites are olive-green in natural light, turning into raspberry red under artificial light. Cat's Eye, so-called because it has a streak of light in the middle, as in the eye of a cat, comes in hues of honey-yellow and apple-green. Other popular stones you might consider are amethysts, garnets, aquamarines and moonstones.

If you don't fancy trying to strike a bargain in the streets, the gem and jewellery shops found in the arcades of five-star hotels are recommended. Others of good repute include **Premadasa & Co** at 560 Galle Road, Colombo 3, tel: 2595178; **Hemachandra Brothers**, 229 Galle Road, Colombo 4, tel: 325147; and **Zam Gems** of 81 Galle Road, Colombo 4, tel: 2589090. The Sri Lanka Gem and Jewellery Exchange (310 Galle Road, Colombo 3) is a government institution with a gem-testing laboratory. Here foreigners can benefit from a free gem-testing service.

You might find cheaper prices elsewhere in the country. For example, in Bentota, Aida Gems and Jewellery (192 Galle Road, Bentota; tel: 03422 75397) provides

Left: handicrafts represent local culture
Right: an array of gemstones

a certificate of authenticity with purchases. And locally crafted, highly fashionable costume jewellery of exquisite design can be purchased at the Stone 'n' String outlets in Liberty Plaza, Majestic City, Crescat as well as at the company's headquarters at 275 R A De Mel Mawatha, Colombo 3; tel: 2301555.

Batiks

Batiks come in any number of attractive colours and patterns and are frequently turned into shirts, sarongs, saris, tablecloths, wall hangings or even curtains. The most popular designs involve motifs of elephants, peacocks and Kandyan dancers. **Laksala**, the government handicraft shop, has an excellent selection of lovely batiks for sale at York Street, Colombo.

Ceramics

Noritake ceramics at bargain-basement prices make excellent purchases. These sets are manufactured in Sri Lanka, and both export-quality and factory seconds with minor flaws are available in a wide array of colours and designs from **Ceylon Ceramics Corporation** (Mon–Fri 9.30am–5.15pm, Sat 9.30am–1.15pm), 696 Galle Road, Colombo 3, tel: 2587526.

Handicrafts

An extensive range of popular handicraft items includes mats, masks, drums, coconut-shell dolls, boxes made from porcupine quills, lace, reed, basket and bambooware, lacquerware, wooden figurines, shell crafts, and silver and brassware. Ubiquitous but nonetheless attractive are the varied representations of Sri Lanka's elephants, in particular painted batik-style or carved from ebony.

If you are shopping for souvenirs, the following outlets, all in Colombo, are good places to begin your search: **Laksala**, York Street, Colombo 1; **Lakmedura**, 113 Dharmapala Mawatha, Colombo 7, tel: 2328900; and **Lakpahana**, 21, Rajakeeya Mawatha, Colombo 7, tel: 2692554. All three stores are open Mon–Fri 9.30am–5.30pm and also on Saturday morning.

Cashew Nuts

This is the fruit Sri Lankans call 'the one which caught God napping'. The story goes that, as this was the last fruit to be created, there was no time to insert the seed before the stroke of midnight. It is for this reason that the cashew seed hangs under the fruit, not inside it. Cashews, either plain or roasted, are sold all over the island, in packets from shops and from stalls on street corners. If you want to give them as a gift, cashews packed in attractive, eye-catching containers are available at the **Expo Shoppe**, Liberty Plaza shopping complex.

Tea

Tea has been synonymous with Sri Lanka for centuries. Even people who have never heard of Sri Lanka are familiar with Ceylon tea, which is popular throughout the world. It is, not suprisingly, the mainstay of the economy on the island.

Tea absorbs moisture very quickly so it must be kept completely dry. Keep your tea leaves in a bottle with the lid tightly screwed on and store it in a cool, dry place. After opening the bottle, replace the cap as soon as possible. If these few rules are observed, the tea will keep well.

Tea for all palates is available, the most highly recommended brand being Orange

Above left: masks are popular handicraft items
Above right: Ceylon tea is famous throughout the world

Pekoe if you like tea without milk, or, if you prefer your cuppa a little stronger, Broken Orange Pekoe. Tea marketed in an incredible and attractive variety of gift packs (created to look like ceramic elephants or miniature wooden tea chests, for example) is available from the many branches of the Mlesna Tea Centre in the Hilton, the main shopping complexes in Colombo, Nuwara Eliya, Galle, Kandy and at the airport. (Mlesna Ceylon Limited, 44 Ward Place, Colombo 7; tel: 2696348; fax: 2697358). Tea Tang (215 1st Division, Colombo 10; tel: 2446214, fax: 2449865) is another speciality tea firm with outlets at the World Trade Centre, Liberty Plaza and the airport.

Spices

An aromatic range of spices – which constitute the very heart of Sri Lankan cuisine – including the likes of cumin and coriander, come packaged in plain plastic packets and also in beautiful gift boxes. Try **The Spice Shop** at Majestic City, Colombo 4, at the Bambalapitiya Junction. Fine spices can also be bought at the Mlesna Tea Centre outlets.

Leather Products

Local craftsmen turn fine-quality leather into belts, shoes, handbags, jackets, coats, wallets, purses, skirts and all sorts of other products. Bespoke shoes cobbled to the individual's specifications cost somewhere in the region of Rs2,000, but prices vary considerably, depending on design, size and how urgently you want the shoes delivered. A number of kiosks close to the Colombo Fort railway station sell leather items. If, however, you're looking for something of better quality, try The Leather Collection at 26 Flower Road, Colombo 7; tel: 2575299.

Antiques

A number of antiques shops in Colombo stock ancient – or at least old – objects including gramophones, clocks and Buddhist statues. **Raux Brothers** at 7 De Fonseka Road, Colombo 5; tel: 5339016; fax: 5339014, and **Treasure Trove** at 247 Galle Road, Mount Lavinia (tel: 2717253) are highly recommended. If you are interested in rooting out antiques (especially furniture) for yourself, visit the antiques stores in the old colonial houses to be found by driving down the Galle Road through Beruwela, Bentota and Ambalangoda. But be warned that it is illegal to export objects that are more than 50 years old without a permit.

Fashions

There are bargains galore to be found if you're looking to buy new clothes. The latest in men's and women's casual fashions for both summer- and winterwear can be found at Odel Unlimited, 5 Alexandra Place, Colombo 7; tel: 2682712. Export-quality goods with many famous brand-name labels are sold here at a fraction of overseas prices.

Home Décor

Several Colombo shops sell items for the modern home. In these outlets you will find unusual gifts such as cushion covers inlaid with the Sinhala or Tamil alphabet, handwoven cotton sarongs, old-fashioned ink

blotters, and colourful doorstops. Exploring these shops is a rewarding way to see an unknown side of local craftsmanship.

Although Barefoot (704 Galle Road, Colombo 3; tel: 2589305) specialises in bright fabrics and unusual gifts, the undoubted leader in fascinating, unexpected items for the home and souvenirs is Paradise Road (213 Dharmapala Mawatha Colombo 7; tel: 2686043). Paradise Road has branches at the Trans Asia Hotel, in the JAIC Hilton mall and at the Gallery Café (2 Alfred House Road, Colombo 3; tel: 2582162).

Above: treasures for sale on the roadside

EATING OUT

If variety is the spice of life, the spices of Sri Lanka will titillate your palate several times over. There are aromatic spices for different curries – tried and tested in recipes that have been handed down from one generation to another. One also has to consider the heritage of dishes bequeathed by traders and conquerors. Old Dutch and Portuguese delicacies such as *bolo fiado* (laminated cake) and *boroa* (semolina biscuits) are an integral part of Sri Lankan cuisine. *Biryani*, a traditional Muslim rice-and-meat dish, and Tamil *thosai* (pancakes) and *vade* (fritters), have also become indigenous to local cooking.

Rice is the staple and there are over 15 varieties in Sri Lanka. A favourite is the red country rice, *kakuluhaal*. This strain is full of vitamins and has a unique nutty flavour, as the grains are left unpolished. White rice, whether the ball-shaped *sambha*, the long-grained *basmati* or the white *milchard*, is widely available. If you want to go native and eat the local rice and curry with your fingers, you should use the right hand only. A bowl of water is provided at the end of the meal for rinsing the fingers.

Rice is used in a variety of dishes. *Kiribath* (milk rice) is a breakfast dish made with rice cooked in coconut cream or fresh milk and spices. This is considered an auspicious meal and is very often eaten during special occasions – on the first of each month, or on welcoming visitors. *Indiappa* (string hoppers) is a Sri Lankan invention that resembles fine noodles. It is made by squeezing a mixture of rice flour (or plain flour) and water through a colander onto bamboo trays and then steam-cooking the mix till it's fluffy.

Appa (hoppers), a type of pancake with crispy edges and made of rice or plain flour with coconut milk and yeast, is a favourite Sri Lankan breakfast dish. String-hopper *biryani* – a lunch or dinner delicacy – is produced by breaking *indiappa* into small pieces and then cooking it with spices, meat and cashew nuts. *Lamprais* is a Dutch variation in which rice and curries are wrapped in banana leaves and steamed with chicken or beef. Lamprais is available at up-market pastry shops (try the Food Courts at Crescat Boulevard and Majestic City).

Lunch packets of rice and curry (usually rice with three vegetable curries and one meat curry) are the mainstay of lunching office workers. They are available in simple cafés throughout Colombo. *Pittu* is ground rice or plain flour mixed with coconut and then steam-cooked in a bamboo container. *Pittu* is eaten with coconut milk, or with meat or fish.

A kind of flimsy pancake, *godamba roti* is a particularly favourite among Muslims. It is fascinating to see this being made as, with each turn of the expert handler's wrist, a small ball of flour becomes longer and flatter. Another popular dish is *watallappan*, the ingredients of which are jaggery (a coarse brown sugar made from the sap of the date palm), eggs, milk and cashew nuts. This is a delicious but rich and heavy dessert.

When it comes to drink, local brews – particularly beer packaged in large bottles – are very popular. Ceylon Breweries' beer is made with water from the hills of Nuwara Eliya and is an invigorating beverage. To get a taste of a really authentic Sri Lankan product, however, try *arrack*. Made from toddy (the sap of the coconut palm tree) and coconut and distilled in large vats, it's the most inexpensive form of alcohol and is widely available. Toddy drunk fresh from the tree is also much enjoyed by Sri Lankans.

For teetotallers, there is a wide array of tangy fruit juices, the most popular being passion fruit and lime. Imported drinks are expensive compared with local products.

Left: making a hopper

The following restaurant recommendations are all in Colombo, which has become an excellent city in which to sample both international cuisine (from a wide array of countries) and typical local dishes. Compared with the cost of eating out in many western capitals, a top-quality meal at one of the best restaurants in Colombo is reasonable in price.

There is a good range of food kiosks (such as those at the Crescat and Majestic City basement food centres) serving good-quality food at low prices, where two could eat well for less than Rs500. Western-style fast-food outlets such as KFC also offer meals for two at less than Rs500. The buffets served in coffee shops at five-star hotels also fall into the inexpensive category. Dining out in hotels, rather than in restaurants, is popular in Colombo, even with local residents. However, as restaurants endeavour to raise their standards, they are now becoming increasingly fashionable.

Grading of these recommended restaurants is based on the average cost of a three-course meal for two people, without drinks. Restaurants add 15 percent government tax and 10 percent service charge to the bill and this has been included in the calculations. Don't let the phrase 'expensive' put you off; it applies in the Sri Lanka context only, since Rs2,500 for two for a gourmet dinner would be inexpensive anywhere else. The addresses of the large hotels can be found on pages 88–89.

Expensive: above Rs2,500
Moderate: Rs1,250 to Rs2,500
Inexpensive: less than Rs1,250.

Restaurants
Sri Lankan
Banana Leaf Restaurant
86 Galle Road, Colombo 4
Tel: 2584403
Friendly, popular local-style restaurant; eat with your fingers from a banana-leaf plate. Inexpensive.

Curry Leaf
Colombo Hilton
Tel: 2544644
A good taste of local cuisine in the Colombo Hilton garden; dinner only. Moderate.

Palmyra Restaurant
Hotel Renuka, 328 Galle Road, Colombo 3
Tel: 2573598
Famous for its Sri Lankan food, complemented by the cuisine of Jaffna; table d'hôte or à la carte; lunch and dinner. Inexpensive.

Rohan's
199 Union Place, Colombo 2
Tel: 2302679
A buffet of local dishes served at lunchtime in the air-conditioned veranda, overlooking a pleasant garden, of a restaurant known for Indian food. Inexpensive.

Chinese
Chinese Dragon
11 Milagiriya Avenue, Colombo 4
Tel: 2503637/2598582
Popular restaurant that serves a spicy blend of Chinese food with a Sri Lankan twist. Whole crab with ginger and garlic is popular; lunch and dinner. Moderate.

Crab Claws
Galadari Hotel
Tel: 2544544
In the corner of the hotel's lobby coffee shop, an eclectic list of good Chinese dishes prepared by a Chinese chef. Moderate.

Emperor's Wok
Colombo Hilton
Tel: 2544644
Five-star, elegant dining. Closed for lunch Friday and all day Sunday. Expensive.

Above: a mouth-watering array of fruit at Kandy market

Flower Drum Restaurant
26 Thurstan Road, Colombo 3
Tel: 2574216
Located in Colombo's expanding restaurant district, this restaurant is popular for its wide variety of Chinese food. Try the hot-plate sizzlers and the lemon chicken. Moderate.

Golden Dragon
Taj Samudra Hotel
Tel: 2446622
Sichuan and Cantonese cuisine. Moderate.

Great Wall
491 Galle Road, Colombo 3
Tel: 2508266
A small restaurant in an office complex near the Bambalapitiya junction. Inexpensive.

Long Feng
Trans Asia Hotel
Tel: 2544200
The place for cuttlefish, especially tasty when stir-fried with mushrooms. Expensive.

Indian
Alhambra
Holiday Inn
Tel: 2422001
Moghul buffet on Friday evening. Moderate.

Navratna
Hotel Taj Samudra
Tel: 2446622
Fine Indian food, cosy setting. Expensive.

Saras
450E, R A de Mel Mawatha, Colombo 3
Tel: 2575226
A taste of two cultures. Both Indian and Chinese dishes are served in a reputable garden-side restaurant. Closed on Monday. Inexpensive.

Rohan's North Indian Cuisine
199 Union Place, Colombo 2
Tel: 2302679
Tasty north Indian food, served in a stylish restaurant. Moderate.

Shanmugas
53/3 Ramakrishna Road, Colombo 6
Tel: 2587629
Vegetarian restaurant, specialising in cuisine from both the north and south of India. Inexpensive.

Indonesian
Bali Restaurant
34 Thurstan Road, Colombo 3
Tel: 2372265
Good Indonesian food. Open evenings only. Moderate.

Japanese
Ginza Hoshen
Colombo Hilton Hotel
Tel: 2544644
Good for *shabu shabu* (hotpot). All ingredients imported from Japan. Exquisite à la carte menu and set dishes. Expensive.

Moshi Moshi Japanese Restaurant
594/2 Galle Road, Colombo 3
Tel: 2500312
Beer garden and *tatami* room. Moderate.

Korean
Han Gook Gwan
25 Havelock Road, Colombo 5
Tel: 2587961
Authentic Korean food. Try the steamboat (buffet). Moderate.

Seafood
Pearl Seafood Restaurant
Ceylon Continental Hotel
Tel: 2421221
Discreet, enjoyable, air-conditioned environment, as well as outdoor seating. Serves a variety of excellent seafood, sometimes to the sounds of a live calypso band. Dinner only. Expensive.

Pier 56
74a Dharmapala Mawatha, Colombo 7.
Tel: 2574384
Good range of seafood and a sushi bar. Fish gaze back at diners from tanks ranged around the restaurant. Sunday lunch buffet. Evenings only except Sunday. Reservations recommended. Moderate.

Sea Fish Restaurant
15 Sir Chittampalam Gardiner Mawatha, Colombo 2
Tel: 2326915
Colombo's oldest (since 1969) fish restaurant, dated ambience but fresh eastern and western seafood dishes. Within walking distance of four five-star hotels. Inexpensive.

Sea Spray Restaurant
Galle Face Hotel
Tel: 2541010
You can dine on a patio overlooking the Indian Ocean or in the cosy indoor atmosphere of this colonial-era hotel. Evenings only. Moderate.

Thai
Sashaka Thai Palace
357 Duplication Road, Colombo 3
Tel: 574998
Pleasant, lively atmosphere for Thai dishes

incorporating local and imported ingredients. Inexpensive.

Siam House
55 Abdul Gaffoor Mawatha, Colombo 3
Tel: 576993
In a 1950s-style house with several dining rooms, the Siam House serves spicy Thai dishes. Moderate.

Western
California Grill
Galadari Hotel
Tel: 544544
Superb views over Galle Face Green and the sea; excellent-quality dishes, many of them prepared at your table by the chef. Evenings only. Expensive.

Chesa Swiss
3 Deal Place A, Colombo 3
Tel: 2573433
Fine dining and immaculate service. Swiss-inspired food and an all-Swiss wine list. Excellent cheese board. Expensive.

German Restaurant
11 Galle Face Court, Colombo 3
Tel: 421577
Ample portions and an atmosphere redolent of a beer cellar. Good draught beer and schnapps. Moderate.

Il Capriccio
29 De Fonseka Road, Colombo 5
Tel: 584663
While Mama does the cooking, her daughter supervises the restaurant; authentic Italian food and wine. Open from 5.30pm except Sundays and *poya* days. Moderate.

Il Ponte
Colombo Hilton
Tel: 2544644
Next to the pool, across the road from the Hilton, you can eat in air-conditioned comfort or in an open-sided space. There's a range of well-presented Italian favourites, and an authentic pizza oven. Moderate.

London Grill
Colombo Plaza Hotel
Tel: 2437437

Left: a traditional lunch of rice and curry

Set in a hidden basement, this place is popular with connoiseurs of traditional dishes beautifully prepared and served. Dinner only. Expensive.

Noblesse
Trans Asia Hotel
Tel: 2544200
French and Mediterranean influence; usually very quiet. Dinner only. Expensive.

Spoons
Colombo Hilton
Tel: 2544644
Spoons is the new name for the Gables restaurant, which has received a complete make-over as well as a different name. Creative contemporary food is served in a stylish lobby restaurant, and the service is excellent. Lunch and dinner. Expensive.

Steak and Grill
Taj Samudra Hotel
Tel: 2446622
Hidden behind the Taj Samudra, specialises in European-inspired cuisine of the kind the name suggests. Expensive.

Bars and Cafes

Cricket Club Café & Bar
34 Queens Road, Colombo 3
Tel: 2501384
Bar, restaurant and veranda-dining with quick service and a varied menu. Lunch and dinner, even on *poya* (Buddhist holiday) days. Moderate.

Deli Market
Level 3, World Trade Centre, Colombo 1
Tel: 2346777
Fast but innovative self-service food, breakfast to dinner; good bar. Inexpensive.

Echelon Pub
Colombo Hilton
Tel: 2544644
Good for pub food and fittings. Moderate.

Gallery Café
2 Alfred House Road, Colombo 3
Tel: 2582162
The former town house of Sri Lanka's top architect, Geoffrey Bawa, this is a café with art, set in a garden. Open for lunch, dinner and drinks. Moderate.

The Pub
Millennium Park, 338 T. B. Jayah Mawatha, Colombo 10
Tel: 681850
Converted from an ancient tea warehouse; plenty of atmosphere; located in a popular theme park with numerous diverse food stalls. Inexpensive.

Rock Café
43 Green Path, Colombo 3
Tel: 565986
With balconies and alcoves in the house and a huge video screen in the garden, this is a very popular, and noisy, night-time hangout for meals or just drinks. Moderate.

Union Bar & Grill Room
Hilton JAIC Tower, 200 Union Place, Colombo 2
Tel: 2300613
Pub and restaurant in a small shopping mall with a modern concept. Closed between lunch and dinner. Moderate.

White Horse Inn
Chatham Street, Colombo 1
Located in an old colonial building, especially popular with young foreigners. Open 10am–11pm, till 3am on Friday and Saturday. Inexpensive.

Left: chillis heat up Sri Lankan food

NIGHTLIFE

Colombo's nightlife includes karaoke bars, discos (which tend to be very crowded on Friday and Saturday nights and can charge up to Rs400 for entrance) and casinos. There is no charge for entry, drinks and food in the casinos where the minimum stake at roulette is either Rs20 or Rs50.

Ballys
14 Dharmapala Mawatha, Colombo 7
Tel: 2573497
Popular casino. Open 24 hours.

Bellagio
430 R. A. De Mel Mawatha, Colombo 3
Tel: 2575271
A bright, popular casino, open 24 hours.

Blue Elephant
Colombo Hilton
Tel: 2544644
This disco is very popular, and often so overcrowded there's barely enough room on the dance floor for Travolta wannabes to strut their stuff. Features include regular theme nights.

Blue Leopard
Grand Oriental Hotel
Tel: 2320391
Popular night club and disco. Open daily 6.30pm–3am.

Colombo 2000
Galadari Hotel
Tel: 2544544
Well-run disco with spacious dance floor, video screen.

Legends
5th Floor, Majestic City, Colombo 4
Tel: 074 515144
This disco can be difficult to find: enter by lift from basement car park. Closed Mon and Tues.

MGM Grand Casino
772 Galle Road, Colombo 4
Tel: 2502268
Open 24 hours and located in a prominent position not far from Majestic City.

Ritz Club
5 Galle Face Terrace, Colombo 3
Tel: 341496
This is a well-known and long-established club, with a VIP room for those who want privacy; open 6pm–4am (until 6am Friday and Saturday).

24-hour Hotel Coffee shops

Although known as coffee shops, these venues are much more varied than the name suggests. They offer daily buffets for breakfast, lunch and dinner and some have *à la carte* dishes available as well.

Many of them also serve late-night snacks, as well as a variety of drinks, and can be a useful standby if you are hungry after a long evening out.

Coffee Shop
Galadari Hotel
Tel: 2544544
Moderate

Emerald
Hotel Ceylon Continental
Tel: 2421221
Moderate

Gardenia
Holiday Inn
Tel: 2422001
Moderate

Lotus Terrace
Colombo Hilton Hotel
Tel: 2544644
Moderate

Ports of Call
Hotel Taj Samudra
Tel: 2446622
Moderate

Taprobane
Colombo Plaza Hotel
Tel: 2437437
Moderate

Summerfields
Trans Asia Hotel
Tel: 2544200
Moderate

CALENDAR OF EVENTS

Sri Lanka has the largest number of official public holidays in the world, so it's a good idea to arm yourself with a local calendar and plan your itinerary accordingly. If you haven't checked specific dates in advance with the Sri Lankan High Commission or embassy in your country, the Tourist Board publishes an annual calendar of events which provides a full listing of all notable dates and holidays. The dates of major Buddhist *Peraheras* (processions) fluctuate annually, according to the lunar calendar.

Of the 26 annual holidays some inevitably fall on a Sunday, which is already a holiday, so employees are entitled to four extra days off. All major events in the Buddhist, Hindu, Muslim and Christian calendars are celebrated as a holiday.

Travelling over a long weekend can be a nuisance because bus and train services are likely to be delayed, overcrowded and, not infrequently, cancelled altogether. In addition to the closure of shops, entertainment houses and business establishments, no alcohol is served in hotels and restaurants on *Poya* (full moon) holidays. If coming on a business visit, remember that people will be out of town and entertainment will be muted. Hotel bars are closed, leaving guests to resort to their minibars.

January

Duruthu Perahera: The Kelaniya Temple near Colombo commemorates the visit of the Buddha to Kelaniya.

Thai Pongal: (14 January) A Hindu harvest festival of the sun god.

February

Independence Day: (4 February) Celebrated with parades, dances, floats and other cultural events.

Navam Perahera: This celebration at the Gangarama Temple in Colombo is establishing itself as an essential item on the tourist calendar. Elephants and dancers form a colourful parade for three nights.

Mahashivaratri: The Hindu festival which commemorates the winning of Lord Shiva by his consort, Parvati, through penance.

March/April

Good Friday/Easter Sunday: The Easter Passion play presented by Roman Catholics in Duwa, near Negombo, is similar to the event in Oberammergau.

April

Sinhala/Hindu New Year: (13–14 April) For the Sinhalese and the Tamils, the island's two main communities, New Year is an occasion to remember age-old traditions, boil milk rice, wear new clothes and visit par-

ents and loved ones. It is a time for merry-making and games. The day prior to the Sinhala and Tamil New Year's Day is also celebrated as a public holiday.

May

May Day: (1 May) Celebrated with huge rallies throughout Colombo.

Vesak: The most important Buddhist celebration, commemorating the birth, enlightenment and death of the Buddha. Homes are filled with bright lights and lanterns. Look out for *pandals*, bamboo pavilions hung with paintings representing scenes from the different lives of the Buddha.

It is also a time for *dansal*, or food donations. Free meals and drinks are offered throughout the island. Temples are usually filled with devotees paying their respects.

The day after the Vesak Full Moon, Poya Day is also a national holiday.

June

Poson: Full Moon Day. Island-wide celebrations commemmorate the arrival of Buddhism to Sri Lanka through the son of Emperor Ashoka.

July/August

Kataragama: The festival at this jungle shrine in southern Sri Lanka includes a *Perahera* (procession). Fire-walking is another traditional feature.

Esala Perahera: This is one of the world's oldest historical pageants, which has been celebrated for several centuries. It is commonly regarded as *the* event of the year, and Kandy comes alive with the throbbing of drums, the tinkling bells of brightly caparisoned elephants and the whirling movements of costumed Kandyan dancers. The *Perahera* continues for 10 consecutive nights and concludes with a 'water cutting' ceremony in which a sword is used to symbolically cut the waters of the Mahaweli River.

Water taken immediately from the spot where the sword divides it is placed in a special pot and kept in Kandy's Temple of the Tooth until the next *Perahera*. A replica of the Buddha's tooth is paraded through the streets on the back of an elephant.

Vel: During this Hindu festival, two enor-

mous black bulls drag a cart through the streets of Colombo. The 6.5-km (4-mile) procession moves at a snail's pace and only reaches its destination at the end of the day.

September/October

The Binara Full Moon *Poya* Day and the Vap Full Moon *Poya* Day in September and October are marked with Buddhist services.

November

Deepavali (Diwali): Hindu homes celebrate the triumph of light over darkness with hundreds of oil lamps to welcome Lakshmi, the goddess of wealth and prosperity.

December

Christmas/New Year: (25 December/1 January). Both are celebrated island-wide with the latter heralded by fire crackers on the stroke of midnight.

This is also the beginning of the auspicious season (December to March) to visit the holy **Adam's Peak**.

In addition to the above festivals, Muslims celebrate the end of the Ramadan fasting month, the Haj festival and the Birthday of Prophet Mohammed. The dates of these festivals vary from year to year.

Left: dancers in the street at Colombo's Vel festival
Above: Kandy comes alive for the Perahera

Practical Information

GETTING THERE

By Air

The majority of visitors arrive by air at Colombo's Bandaranaike International Airport, situated near the town of Katunayake, 32km (20 miles) north of Colombo.

The national airline, which used to be known as Air Lanka, became Sri Lankan Airlines in 1999, following a partnership deal with the award-winning Emirates Airlines of Dubai.

The alliance with Emirates has resulted in a number of changes in an effort to persuade long-haul passengers, such as those travelling from Europe to Australia, to use UL and stop over in Colombo. New aircraft have been introduced, first-class status has been abolished in favour of an improved business class and several new routes have been added.

Sri Lankan Airlines features daily non-stop flights to and from Europe, and non-stop flights to and from the Far East. The airline also serves the Maldives, the Middle East, the Far East and India. The Indian gateways are Bombay, Madras, Delhi, Bangalore, Hyderabad, Cochin, Tiruchchirappalli and Trivandrum.

Other airlines serving Colombo include Aeroflot, Cathay Pacific, Emirates, Gulf Air, Indian, Jet Airways, Kuwait Air, LTU, Malaysian, Oman Air, Pakistan International Airlines, Qatar Air, Royal Jordanian, Sahara, Saudi, Singapore and Thai.

Due to Sri Lanka's popularity as a holiday destination, it is possible to reduce the normally high airfares from Europe by buying a package of flight and hotel through a travel agent. Of course, you don't have to stay in the hotel for the entire duration of your visit, and there's no reason why you can't explore the country independently. For the independent traveller, last-minute tickets at a reduced price are available at some international airports, and through ticket consolidators. On arrival, you might be asked to show that you have an air ticket out of Sri Lanka by the immigration authorities.

The airport is one of the best in the Indian subcontinent: clean, brightly lit and comfortable. There are several duty-free shops in the departure lounge, including some that sell gold. Visitors can buy their duty-free quota of alcohol on arrival instead of bringing it with them.

The best way to get from the airport to Colombo is by taxi, which can be booked at a desk in the arrival hall, after you've been through customs. The cost should be about Rs1,000. There is no scheduled airport coach service.

By Sea

The days of regular voyages by passenger ships to Colombo are long gone. However, the city has become quite popular with visiting cruise liners. Although no cruise line company actually begins or ends an itinerary at Colombo, it is often possible to join or leave a cruise there by prior arrangement. Cruise liners call during the months of October to April as part of an Indian Ocean Cruise.

The *Marco Polo* and the *Queen Elizabeth II* visit every year, and Colombo is also included on the itinerary of the

Left: a local form of transport
Right: warm days, balmy nights

luxury Seabourn cruise line. Since cruise ships stay at the port for a whole day, it is possible for passengers to go ashore to explore Colombo and even make a day trip to Kandy. It is a good way to see a little of Sri Lanka, and might even tempt you back for a longer holiday.

Information about cruises is available from specialist travel agents. Some freighters also carry passengers – contact the shipping lines for information. Yachts have been known to drop anchor, usually at the port of Galle in the south, during round-the-world voyages.

TRAVEL ESSENTIALS

When to Visit
For the west and south coast, the best time to visit is between November and March, when the seas are calm and the weather is quite good, though there may be occasional showers. This is the winter season, as in Europe, and accommodation rates are at their highest at this time. December and January are popular months and, unless you book ahead, you might find some of the hotels are busy. April through October is the best time to visit the east coast but, as a result of trouble spilling over from the north, tourists are not encouraged to go to the eastern province. Check with your embassy for the latest update.

Sri Lanka's two monsoons come from different directions. From May to July the southwest monsoon brings rain to the west and south; the northeast monsoon hits the north and east from November to January.

March/April is the hottest time, but the hills are lovely at this time of year. Accommodation in hill resorts such as Nuwara Eliya can be difficult to find in these months.

Visas and Passports
Nationals of 64 countries, including Australia, Canada, France, Germany, Japan, New Zealand, the UK and the USA, do not need visas for stays of up to one month if arriving as tourists. Check with your travel agent because more countries are periodically added to the list. It is important to remember that visas are not issued to those who arrive from countries not on the list. Visas should

be obtained from a Sri Lankan consular office, or through a British consular office if there are no Sri Lankan offices.

Visa extensions can be issued in a day at the office of the Department of Immigration and Emigration at the end of the road running towards the sea beside Majestic City (Station Road, Bambalapitiya, Colombo 4; tel: 2597511). The charge for a visa is usually the same amount that the tourist's country charges a Sri Lankan visiting that nation. Proof of money spent in the country may be requested, so be prepared to show encashment certificates of foreign exchange, as well as your ticket to leave the country on a specific date.

Vaccinations
Yellow-fever vaccinations are essential if you are coming from an infected country. Immunisation against cholera and hepatitis A is advised. Anti-malaria pills are recommended if you visit rural areas.

Customs
Those bringing in more than US$10,000 or its equivalent should declare it at customs on arrival. Valuable equipment, gems and jewellery should also be declared.

Tourists should go through the green channel if there is nothing to declare. Duty-free allowances include 1.5 litres of spirits, two bottles of wine, 200 cigarettes or 50 cigars and a small quantity of perfume. Travel souvenirs not exceeding US$250 in value are also allowed in without payment of duty. Import of dangerous drugs, firearms, obscene literature and pictures is an offence. Illegal-drug importers can be executed.

On departure, all bags are X-rayed at the entrance to the airport, then hand-searched before check-in. This is done by airport security personnel, watched by customs officers looking for illegal exports. It is illegal to export antiques (ie, an item over 50 years old) without a permit; or more than 3kg (6.6lbs) of tea, unless duty is paid. Batteries, radios and electronic equipment are best checked-in rather than carried by hand. If you have bought gems, keep the receipt to show to customs officers. You can convert your Sri Lankan currency at the departure lounge.

practical information

Climate

In Colombo, the average annual temperature is 27°C (81°F); in Kandy at an altitude of 488m (1,600ft), it is 20°C (68°F); and in Nuwara Eliya, nestled high in the hills at 1,890m (6,200ft), the temperature averages 16°C (61°F). The highest temperatures are usually reached between March and June, while November to January is the coolest period.

Note that the difference between the 'hot' and 'cool' seasons is a matter of a few degrees. The ocean remains a constant 27°C (81°F) throughout the year.

Clothing

Casual clothes of light cotton or terry cotton are recommended; if you're heading for the hill country, where temperatures at night can drop to 10°C (50°F), remember to bring a sweater. It's advisable to have a good insect-repellent, and sunscreen lotion with a high sun-protection factor (SPF). The sun is hotter than it seems and without adequate protection, sunburn resulting from prolonged exposure, especially at beach resorts, can lead to an unpleasant holiday. Drink lots of liquid as the heat and humidity cause you to lose water through sweat. Bottled mineral water can be bought easily everywhere.

Electricity

Electricity is 230 volts at 50 cycles AC. Some hotels have 110-volt outlets for shavers. The plugs are normally the round type with a square pin as used in newer hotels. A multisocket plug will be helpful.

Time Differences

Sri Lanka is six hours ahead of Greenwich Mean Time (GMT) following the time change introduced in 1996.

GETTING ACQUAINTED

Government and Economy

Sri Lanka is a parliamentary democracy with an elected executive president. The 225 members of parliament are elected on a complicated proportional voting system.

The basis of the economy is agriculture and some rice is still imported. Incredibly, the island imports canned fish. Tea, rubber, coconut and agricultural products account for about a third of the island's total exports; the rest are mainly industrial.

The per capita income of the 20 million inhabitants is more than US$700. The people of Sri Lanka enjoy free education and health care, and a very impressive literacy rate of 92 percent – one of the highest in Asia. It's also worth noting that the infant mortality rate is one of the continent's lowest.

Life expectancy is 69 years for males and 74 years for females.

The rate of population growth has been calculated at 1.2 percent. Some 75 percent of the population reside in rural areas.

The population is made up of the following groups: 74 percent Sinhalese, 12.7 percent Sri Lanka Tamils, 5.5 percent Indian Tamils, 7 percent Sri Lanka Moors and 0.8 percent described as 'others'.

Above: locals play a Sri Lankan board game at a roadside

indeed will often ask you for a copy if you take a photo of them; don't agree to their request and then forget to send the picture.

When entering temples, remove your shoes and headgear as a sign of respect. Women should not wear short skirts, shorts or transparent blouses when entering temples. Monks should not be touched; if you meet one and wish to show respect, raise both hands in a prayer-like manner to just below your chin. Remember to be sensitive to local religious customs.

MONEY MATTERS

Currency and Credit Cards
The Sri Lanka rupee is divided into 100 cents. Coins and notes come in various different denominations, up to Rs1000. Check the newspapers daily for bank rates, but use this only as a rough guide as the actual amount you will receive is a little less. Some banks charge a fee for changing travellers' cheques, so check the exchange rates and bank charges before changing money. You will get more rupees for travellers' cheques than you will for the same amount of cash. Rates of exchange offered at hotels are generally lower than at banks.

All leading credit cards are accepted at major establishments; check in advance if you have any doubts.

Tipping
Hotels and restaurants add a 10 percent service charge and a 15 percent government tax to your bill. You can leave an additional tip (about 5 percent) for the waiter at your discretion, if service has been particularly good. Rs20 per bag carried by porters is a good tip. For auto-rickshaws (three-wheeler taxis), a few rupees is a sufficient tip. For taxis with air-conditioning, anything up to 10 percent of the (metered) fare will suffice. For the driver of a vehicle hired for a tour, add 5 to 10 percent of the agreed price.

Airport Tax
The departure tax of Rs1500 is included in your ticket. If you are meeting someone on an arriving plane, access to the airport waiting area costs Rs130.

Sinhala is the language spoken by most of the population. The constitution designates Sinhala and Tamil as the official languages and English as the 'link' language. English is widely spoken, particularly in the mercantile and tourist sectors.

Religion
In Sri Lanka, Buddhists constitute 69.3 percent of the population, Hindus 15.5 percent, Muslims 7.6 percent, Christians 7.5 percent and others 0.1 percent.

Geography
Sri Lanka is 445km (277 miles) long and 225km (140 miles) wide. The coastline is over 1,600km (1,000 miles) long, the landmass occupies 65,610 sq km (25,332 sq miles), about the size of the Netherlands and Belgium combined. The highest mountain is Pidurutalagala (2,524m8,281ft). Sri Jayewardenepura-Kotte is the administrative capital, Colombo the commercial capital.

Culture and Customs
Sri Lankans are a very friendly and helpful people, but beware of touts who prey on tourists. Making friends is easy and do not be surprised if a local invites you home for a meal. The people are not camera shy and

Above: Sri Lankans are a friendly people
Right: the Viceroy Special steam train

Black Market

The black-market rate is only a few cents more than the official one and not worth the risk involved; it's a better idea to use the banks or an official money changer. In casinos, US dollars will be changed at a better rate than in a bank, but the chips you receive to play with will, depending on your winnings, have to be exchanged for cash.

Business Hours

Government offices are open 9am–5pm Mon-Fri, private offices from 8am to 5pm. Shops are open 9am–6pm on weekdays and half day Sat. The majority of banks are open 9am–3pm on weekdays but some have longer hours. Seylan Bank closes at 8pm and is also open half day Sat, 9am–11am.

GETTING AROUND

Taxis

Taxis charge between Rs25–30 per kilometre travelled while auto-rickshaws are slightly less at about Rs20–25.

Radio taxis have reliable meters, but with auto-rickshaws it is best to get an idea of the distance and agree on a price with the driver before embarking on your journey.

Radio-controlled taxis, GNTC (tel: 2688688) and Kangaroo Cabs (tel: 2501502) charge Rs40 per kilometre.

Trains

Train services are reliable and the inter-city expresses are recommended. Second- and third-class tickets are usually available. A limited number of services sell first-class tickets. All enquiries regarding train times and bookings can be made at the Fort Railway Station, tel: 2434215. Furthermore, fares are very reasonable. The 116-km (72-

mile) journey from Colombo to Kandy on the Inter City costs Rs100, a third-class ticket on a normal train costs Rs35.

The *Viceroy Special* steam train can be chartered for private trips and sometimes seats are available on trips arranged by travel agents. The steam-train tours are organised in co-operation with the Sri Lanka Railways by JF Tours & Travels (Ceylon) Ltd, 189 New Bullers Road, Colombo 4; tel: 2587996; fax: 2580507.

Buses

Public buses are very basic and not exactly comfortable, but they are cheap. The bus fare from Colombo to Kandy is less than the third-class fare by rail. There are also a few luxury air-conditioned Inter City buses.

Cars

The best way to get around is to either hire a hotel taxi or arrange a chauffeur-driven car through a travel agent. The latter is cheaper than a self-drive car.

Many Sri Lankan drivers fail to acknowledge elementary road etiquette, and although the mood in the country is generally relaxed, patience is not the most common virtue of Sri Lankans behind a wheel. You would not be far wrong if you were to assume that bus and taxi drivers keep their fingers permanently pressed on the horn. Even if you are a very patient, careful driver, you will probably want to leave the navigation of roads and traffic to locals.

Private cars can be hired for about Rs20 a kilometre. Self-drive cars are available at about Rs25 per kilometre, but a refundable deposit of Rs5,000 will be requested. Usually the car comes with a virtually empty fuel tank so you will need to fill up at the nearest petrol station.

You are obliged to register your international driving licence at the Automobile Association office next to the Holiday Inn in Galle Face, Colombo 3, (tel: 2421528), before you hire a car.

Motorbikes

The adventurous may like to rent motorbikes. A wide selection of the latest models are available from Goldwing, 346 Deans Road, Colombo 10 (tel: 2698787).

ACCOMMODATION

Sri Lanka has more than 10,000 hotel rooms, of which 2,200 in Colombo are in the five-star category. All of the five-star hotels and a few of the cheaper options are listed here. Five-star hotels tend to charge from US$120 per night for a single/double occupancy, although if you specifically ask for a discount, you might just get rooms for less.

A room on a hotel's executive floor guarantees the client access to the executive lounge with breakfast and evening happy-hour drinks included. Medium-range hotels charge in the region of US$45 to US$65, which is comparable to the range for good hotels elsewhere in the world.

All hotels include a 10 percent service charge and a 15 percent VAT in the customer's bill.

Five-Star Hotels in Colombo

Ceylon Continental
Janadhipathi Mawatha, Colombo 1
Tel: 2421221; fax: 2447326
e-mail: hotel@ceyloncontinental.com
This was the first five-star hotel in Sri Lanka. Overlooks the Indian Ocean at one end of Galle Face Green. An executive floor.

Colombo Hilton
Lotus Road, Colombo 1
Tel: 2544644; fax: 2544657
e-mail: hilton@sri.lanka.net
The liveliest of the city's five-star hotels with seven restaurants, a pub, a karaoke room and a disco. Several executive floors.

Colombo Plaza
Stuart Place, Galle Road, Colombo 3
Tel: 2437437; fax: 2442980
e-mail: bc@thecolomboplaza.lk

A much-loved favourite among regulars, but it does have a dim, dated air, despite the addition of a glittering new lobby.

Galadari Hotel
Lotus Road, Colombo 1
Tel: 2544544; fax: 2544585
e-mail: galadari@sri.lanka.net
website: www.sri.lanka.net/galadari
In previous incarnations a Meridian, and then a Marriott, this establishment is now 100-percent locally managed and staffed. It's very smart and is an ideal venue for the business or independent traveller.

Trans Asia Hotel
Sir Chittampalam Gardiner Mawatha,
Colombo 2
Tel: 2544200; fax: 2449184
email: tahasia@sri.lanka.net
Has beautiful Sri Lankan granite floors and Kabok stones, and is well-placed on the edge of the Beira Lake. One executive floor.

Taj Samudra
Galle Face, Colombo 3
Tel: 2446622; fax: 2446348
e-mail: taj@sri.lanka.net
The décor in the lobby of this 400-room property is highly unusual, and the light fixtures are designed to look like the inside of a Sinhala ancestral home (*walawwa*). The swimming pool at the rear is surrounded by a beautiful garden. One executive floor.

Other Colombo Hotels

Galle Face
2 Kollupitiya Road, Colombo 3
Tel: 2541010; fax: 2541072
e-mail: gfh@diamond.lanka.net
One of the oldest hotels in Asia and a gracious relic of the city's colonial past. First

established in 1864, the Galle Face Hotel is the only seaside hotel in the heart of Colombo. Room rates start from US$55 with discounts for non-smokers.

Renuka
328 Galle Road, Colombo 3
Tel: 2573598; fax: 2574137
e-mail: renukahotel.com
A small and elegant 79-room hotel. Rates start from US$42.

Mount Lavinia
Hotel Road, Mount Lavinia
Tel: 2715221; fax: 2738228
e-mail: lavinia@sri.lanka.net
Once the residence of a British governor. Offers beautiful views of the Mount Lavinia beach. Rates start from US$55.

Other Recommended Hotels

Bandarawela
The Bandarawela Hotel
Tel: 05722 31190
Built in 1893 but with an atmosphere redolent of the tranquil 1930s, with glassed-in terrace, deep sofas and beds complete with brass knobs. US$55

Bentota
Bentota Beach Hotel
Tel: 03422 75176; fax: 03422 75179
e-mail: bbh@keells.com
Comfortable hotel right on the beach. On the site of a fort, beautifully refurbished with rooms facing the sea and the lagoon; glittering *à la carte* restaurant. US$110

Saman Villas
Aturuwella
Tel: 03422 75435; fax: 03422 75433
Member of the 'Small Luxury Hotels of the World'. 27 villas, all facing the beach. Perfect for spoiling yourself. US$200

Dambula
Kandalama Hotel
Tel: 06622 84100; fax: 06622 84109
Designed by the Sri Lankan architect Geoffrey Bawa, this stylish hotel is built around the Kandalama Rock. Rooms are small but offer beautiful views of the Kanalama Wewa and the forest. US$150

Galle
Lighthouse Hotel
Tel: 09122 23744; fax: 09122 24201
e-mail: lighthousehotel@lanka.com.lk
New, but with all the glamour of a grand hotel by the sea. US$250

Amangalla
Tel: 09122 33388 Fax: 09122 33355
In Galle Fort, the former New Oriental is once again a byword for luxury thanks to a huge renovation project. US$400

Hikkaduwa
Coral Gardens Hotel
Tel: 09122 77023
On a lovely beach offering trips to view the corals. Pool and air-conditioned rooms. Rates start at around US$60.

Kandy
Queens Hotel
Tel: 0812 233290; fax: 0812 232079
Dating from the 19th century, but recently refurbished and overlooking the Temple of the Tooth and the Kandy lake. US$50

Nuwara Eliya
The Tea Factory, Kandapola
Tel:0522 229600; fax: 0522 229606
e-mail: teafactory@slt.lk
Former 1930s tea factory which is is now a luxury hotel. Good food. US$85

Sigiriya
Sigiriya Village Hotel
Tel: 066 31803
e-mail: hotelssv@sltnet.lk
Wonderful views and exotic garden; 124 chalet-style rooms. Blissfully relaxing.

Unawatuna
Unawatuna Beach Resort
Parangiyawatte
Tel: 0914 380549
Fairly basic but peaceful with year-round bathing in idyllic bay. Has 62 rooms.

Yala
Yala Village Hotel
Tel: /fax: 0115 373305
Getaway near jungle, sea and lagoon. US$70.

Left: Mount Lavinia Hotel

Rented Accommodation

Fully serviced apartments are available in Colombo for short-term stays, with rents around US$2,000 a month.

Crescat Residencies
Lobby 2-B; 75 Galle Road, Colombo 3
Tel: 5530684; fax: 5556260
e-mail: cresales@sri.lanka.net

Hilton JAIC Tower
200 Union Place, Colombo 2
Tel: 5344644; fax: 5344648

HEALTH & EMERGENCIES

Hygiene

Except in reputable hotels, avoid water and salads. It's advisable to drink only bottled table water, beer or soft drinks. Likewise, it is prudent to stick to those fruits that can be washed and peeled. Cut-fruits sold by street vendors should be avoided.

Pharmacies

Most well-known medicines from the West are available from pharmacies. The government-run Osusala pharmacy near Colombo Town Hall (tel: 2694716), is open 24 hours a day. You will find other Osusala pharmacies throughout the island and it shouldn't be hard to find privately owned pharmacies in the towns.

Doctors

Hotels and even small guesthouses keep details of nearby doctors who will attend their guests as required. Charges for a hotel visit will be modest.

Hospitals

Iif you have an accident of any kind in Colombo you should go to the accident service (tel: 2691111) of the General Hospital at Regent Street, Colombo 7.

There are also several reliable private hospitals in Colombo that offer outpatient services. Nawaloka Hospital at 23 Saugathodaya Mawatha, Colombo 2, tel: 2544444, and Durdan's Hospital at 3 Alfred Place, Colombo 3, tel: 2575205, are recommended.

COMMUNICATIONS & NEWS

Postal Services

Your hotel will post your letters for you – and, rest assured, the mail service is fairly efficient. If you are sending valuables, it's a good idea to register the package. The General Post Office (tel: 2326203) is open 6 days a week. Other post offices in Colombo are at Cinnamon Gardens, Kollupitiya (tel: 2573160, 7am–7pm Monday–Friday, 9am–7pm Saturday and 8am–10pm Sunday and public holidays), and at Wellawatte (tel: 2588652, 7am–6pm Monday–Saturday, 8am–10pm Sunday and public holidays).

Telephone

Major hotels have international direct-dial (IDD) facilities. If you would rather make your calls without the hotel's mark up, buy phone cards from general shops and use a card-phone for direct-dial overseas calls. Mobile phones are available to rent for short periods through the leading hotels.

The IDD code when calling Sri Lanka from overseas is 94. To call Colombo from overseas, dial 94 11 and then the number. For all Sri Lanka numbers which have 0 in front (such as Bentota 03422, and mobile numbers like 077), do not dial 0 when phoning from overseas (thus 94 34, 94 74, 94 77). When calling a Colombo number from elsewhere in Sri Lanka, dial 011 first.

Internet

Visitors can surf the internet at any of the independent cyber-cafés in Colombo at rates starting from Rs1 per minute, or otherwise at the British Council for Rs750 for 10 hours of internet access. The following cyber-venues are recommended:

The Café@inter.net
491 Galle Road, Colombo 3
Tel: 4521902; fax: 508616
e-mail: cafe@isplanka.lk

Multimedia Centre
British Council, 49 Alfred House Gardens, Colombo 3
Tel: 2581171; fax: 2587079

practical information

Senkada
466 Union Place, Colombo 2
Tel: 4793111
e-mail: business_center@senkada.lk
Open 24 hours.

Photo processing
The following colour-print lab is open 24 hours a day.
Senkada
466 Union Place, Colombo 2
Tel: 4793111

Media
There are three morning English-language newspapers: the government-run *Daily News,* and the independent *The Island* and *The Daily Mirror.* There are four English-language papers on Sunday: the state-controlled *Sunday Observer,* and the privately-run *Sunday Times, Sunday Island* and *Sunday Leader.*

Foreign papers such as the *International Herald Tribune,* the *Asian Wall Street Journal* and some British papers are available the day after publication at hotel bookshops and at Vijitha Yapa Bookshop at Crescat Boulevard, tel: 5510100.

One radio station and two TV stations are state-owned, the others are independent. BBC and CNN news programmes are available round the clock at hotels. Many Western shows are broadcast on the eight TV channels. English news on the state-controlled Rupavahini TV starts at 9pm nightly. On the radio, the local English-language news is at 6.45am, 1.15pm, 6.15pm and 8.45pm. You need a short-wave radio to hear the BBC World Service.

USEFUL INFORMATION

Tourist Offices
The Tourist Board's information centre is at 78 Stuart Place, Colombo 3, tel: 2437059, 2437060; email: ctbch@sri.lanka.net; website: http//www.lanka.net/ctb. The office is open on weekdays 8.30am–4.45pm, including *Poya* (Buddhist holidays). On Saturday, Sunday and public holidays, it is open till 12.30pm. There is also a useful information counter in the arrival hall at the airport.

SPORT

Cricket is popular in Sri Lanka. The season begins in September and ends with the finals in April. Sri Lanka is a member of the International Cricket Conference and Test matches are played against the leading countries. Visitors can enjoy the benefits of temporary membership at most clubs. Colombo Cricket Club, 31 Maitland Crescent, Colombo 7, tel: 2691025, is recommended.

The 18-hole golf course at Nuwara Eliya (tel: 0522 223833), has temporary memberships. Or you can play at the Royal Colombo Golf Club, Model Farm Road, Colombo 8; tel: 2695431; fax: 2687592. There is a new club near Kandy that welcomes visitors: Victoria Golf Club, Rajawella, Kandy; tel/fax: 0602 800249; e-mail: victoria@sltnet.lk

For rowing enthusiasts, temporary membership is available at Colombo Rowing Club, 51/1 Sir Chittampalam Gardiner Mawatha, Colombo 2, tel: 2433758.

Underwater Safaris Ltd, 25 Barnes Place, Colombo 7, tel: 2694012, offers wreck and reef diving expeditions at Hikkaduwa on the south coast. A range of water-sports is available at some south-coast hotels and at Negombo on the west coast.

FURTHER READING

Insight Guide: Sri Lanka, Apa Publications, 1999. Revamped and updated, with brand-new maps, travel tips and essays.
History of Sri Lanka, K.M. de Silva, Vijitha Yapa Publications, 2003.

Right: a warm welcome

ACKOWLEDGEMENTS

Photography	**Dominic Sansoni** *and*
Pages 24B, 25, 28, 41T, 47, 49, 57, 70	**Gemunu Amarasinghe**
8/9	**Roland Ammon**
80	**J G Anderson**
10	**P R Anthonis Collection**
14	**Philip Baldeus, A True and Exact**
	Description... of Ceylon 1703
73	**Alain Evrard**
22B	**Manfred Gottschalk**
43, 52	**Dallas & John Heaton**
45	**Rainer Krack**
13, 26T	**KVJ de Silva Collection**
55, 71	**Philip Little**
30, 32, 33, 35, 38, 50, 62T, 62B, 69, 81	**R Ian Lloyd**
22T	**Jonathan Pile/Impact**
21, 37, 39, 44, 48, 56, 75, 82, 85, 86, 91	**Lesley Player**
5, 59, 61T	**G P Reichelt**
15B	**The Senanayake Family Collection**
20, 34, 74, 76, 78	**Tom Tidball**
11	**Bill Wassman**
36, 41B, 42, 46, 51, 53, 61B, 63, 66	**Vijitha Yapa**
Cover	**Michael Busselle/Corbis**
Title page	**G P Reichelt**
Cartography	**Berndston & Berndston**
	Keith Brook

INDEX